For Julian, Elliot, Louis and Sophie

Julie Macfie Sobol & Ken Sobol

LAKE ERIE

A PICTORIAL HISTORY

The BOSTON
MILLS PRESS

A BOSTON MILLS PRESS BOOK

©Julie Macfie Sobol and Ken Sobol, 2004

NATIONAL LIBRARY OF CANADA CATALOGUING IN PUBLICATION

Sobol, Julie Macfie, 1936-
    Lake Erie: a pictorial history / Julie Macfie Sobol and Ken Sobol.

Includes bibliographical references and index.
ISBN 1-55046-361-6

1. Erie, Lake, Region—History. 2. Erie, Lake—History. 3 Erie,
Lake, Region—History—Pictorial works. 4. Erie, Lake—History—Pictorial
works. I. Sobol, Ken II. Title.
FC3095.L335S62 2004   971.3'3   C2003-906838-2

PUBLISHER CATALOGING-IN-PUBLICATION DATA (U.S.)

Sobol, Julie Macfie, 1936-
    Lake Erie: a pictorial history / Julie Macfie Sobol and Ken Sobol.
-1st ed.
[224]p. : photos. ; cm.
Includes bibliographical references and index.
Summary: A portrait of daily life, industry and commerce on Lake Erie.
Chapters cover the lake's prehistory, its early settlement, its role in the
War of 1812, its economic boom from 1815 to 1880, the High Industrial period
from 1880 to 1945, its history of dramatic storms and shipwrecks, and fire and
ice catastrophes, its recreational history, and its wealth of flora and fauna.

ISBN 1-55046-361-6

1. Erie, Lake, Region—History. 2. Erie, Lake—History. 3 Erie,
Lake, Region—History—Pictorial works. 4. Erie, Lake—History—Pictorial
works. I. Sobol, Ken. II. Title.
971.3/3 21   FC3095.L335S62   2004

Published by BOSTON MILLS PRESS
132 Main Street, Erin, Ontario, Canada N0B 1T0
Tel 519-833-2407   Fax 519-833-2195
e-mail: books@bostonmillspress.com   www.bostonmillspress.com

In Canada: Distributed by Firefly Books Ltd.
66 Leek Cresent, Richmond Hill, Ontario, Canada L4B 1H1

In the United States: Distributed by Firefly Books (U.S.) Inc.
P.O. Box 1338, Ellicott Station, Buffalo, New York, USA 14205

Design: Sue Breen and Chris McCorkindale
        McCorkindale Advertising & Design

Printed in Canada

The publisher acknowledges for the financial support of our publishing
program the Canada Council, the Ontario Arts Council, and the
Government of Canada through the Book Publishing Industry Development
Program (BPIDP).

PHOTOS:
Page 1: High Level Bridge, Cleveland, 1940
Page 2: Stanley Beach Casino, Port Stanley, Ontario, c. 1910
Page 6: The lake at Port Dover, Ontario, c. 1910

Front Cover:
Top Left: The Boblo boat, Detroit dock, c. 1910
Top Middle: The Age of the Flapper, on the lake, late twenties
Top Right: Niagara Falls
Middle Left: Ellicott Square, Buffalo, 1900
Middle Middle: Tonawanda, New York harbour, 1895
Middle Right: Grass pike, Port Dover, Ontario, 1907
Bottom Middle: Port Burwell, Ontario harbor 1915
Bottom Right: Defense of Fort Stephenson, near Sandusky, Ohio, 1812

Back Cover:
Top Left: Inscription Rock, Kelleys Island
Top Middle: Smelt run, Long Point
Top Right: Queen's Own Rifles, 1866
Middle Left: Amateur baseball championship, Cleveland, 1914
Middle Right: Storm at Port Dover
Bottom Left: *City of Detroit III*, 1913
Bottom Right: Log rafters, Tonawanda, 1867

LAKE ERIE

Table of Contents

LAKE ERIE
Acknowledgments

Our daughter, Corry Sobol, took time from her busy life to travel with us on occasion, and to take several pictures for the book. She comes first. Others to whom we feel indebted for going out of their way to help include, in no particular order: Shannon and Brian Prince, Jane Penvose, Ron Williamson, Peter Knechtel, Annita Andrick, Dave Mason, Ian Bell, Bill Yeager, Bob Graham, John McGarvey, Nancy Cruickshank, Rob Cromwell, Hilda Deak, Stephen Harding, Kevin Harding and George E. Pond.

In the course of our research we contacted a number of companies closely connected with the early history of the lake. Chris Edwards, editor of the *Walkerville Times*, Dan Feicht from Cedar Point Park, Liz O'Neill at Pelee Island Winery, Cathy Cornell at the Sherwin-Williams Company, Dennis "Mr. 57" Jackson from Heinz Foods, Fran Breitner of Libbey Glass, Ellen Thompson from Laura Secord, and Debra Moore of the Hudson's Bay Archives all supplied material we could have obtained nowhere else.

Sara Cox, Virginia Anger, Honnie Busch, Jane Davies, Carrie Walmsley, John Docker, Douglas Flood, John Furman, Marion Grimes, Kirt Gross, Erin Wilson, Arthur Pegg, Frank and Nancy Prothero, John Conlin and Janet Wetter, Evelyn Runions, Jim Murphy, Bruce Milner, Viswanath Gurram, Stewart Boden, Ron Davidson, Bob Garcia, Henrietta O'Neill, Jay McKiee, Audrey Hoskin and Roland Baumann each lent a very useful hand, and to all of them we are grateful.

We would also like to tip our hats to our ever-available and patient tech people—William Sanchez, Greg Clarke, John Sobol, and Jane Sobol.

Finally, whenever we mentioned our work-in-progress to someone in the publishing business, they would almost always respond, "That's a Boston Mills book if I've ever heard one." And so it is. For that we have to salute the enthusiasm of that old Lake Erie boy John Denison.

Port Burwell Harbor, c. 1915 *Port Burwell Marine Museum*

A SNAPSHOT OF THE LAKE

We were chatting with a German writer we'd recently met when one of us happened to mention that we lived on Lake Erie. A look of incredulous delight appeared on his face. "Not Lake Erie!" he cried. "You come from Lake Erie? That's incredible! I can't believe it! You know, I never thought it was a real place until I grew up! You must know John Maynard!"

"Well, not really. See, it's a big place," we started to explain. But he wasn't inquiring about a possible mutual acquaintance; he had in mind an epic poem of courage and death on the lake by the nineteenth-century poet and novelist Theodor Fontane. As a schoolboy, our new acquaintance had been required to memorize the entire sixty lines. "You must have heard of it," he insisted. "Everybody has," with which he launched into a powerful, you might almost say Germanic, rendition of the opening stanzas:

Wer ist John Maynard?

John Maynard war unser Steuermann,
Aushielt er, bis er das Ufer gewann,
Er hat ein gerettet, er trägt die Kron,
Er starb für uns, unsre Liebe sein Lohn.
John Maynard.

[*Who is John Maynard?*

John Maynard was our pilot true
To safety's shores he brought us through
He saved our lives, our noble king
He died for us; his fame we sing.
John Maynard.]

He went on to summarize the tragic story of *die Schwalbe* (the *Swallow*) a sumptuous sidewheeler that sets out from Detroit for Buffalo, its decks crowded with carefree holidaymakers. The steamer flies swiftly across Lake Erie (*die* Schwalbe *fliegt über den Eriesee*), but as it nears its destination a fire breaks out. Though panic seizes the passengers and crew, Maynard remains calm. With the wheelhouse engulfed in flames, he steers the burning boat onto the shores of Buffalo. The terrified passengers fling themselves over the side to safety and the crew follows, all but our noble helmsman, who, in true Victorian hero fashion, perishes in the conflagration.

It never happened, of course. There never was a helmsman named John Maynard, or a crowded paddle steamer called the *Swallow*, or a happy-go-lucky excursion from Detroit with a frantic dash to safety at Buffalo. A little research revealed that the

9

One source for Alger's poem may be the tragic loss of the sidewheeler *Erie*, built in 1836 and renowned as the fastest lake vessel of her day. On August 9, 1841, the *Erie* departed Buffalo for Chicago full of Swiss and German immigrants. Less than 20 miles out, off Silver Creek on the American side, the boat fell prey to that grimmest of maritime catastrophes in the age of wooden vessels — an uncontrollable fire. In no time, high winds whipped up a seagoing inferno. Of the more than two hundred aboard, only twenty-nine survived. *Historical Collections of the Great Lakes, Bowling Green State University*

celebrated ballad is a pastiche of several genuine Lake Erie disasters, cobbled together in 1861 by the Dr. Feelgood of exuberant nineteenth-century America, Horatio Alger Jr. Apparently Fontane came across Alger's melodramatic verses at some point and was inspired to try his own, more eloquent, version. (The poem became so universally popular that in one of his stories, published in 1912, Stephen Leacock automatically assumed his readers would recognize a reference. When his mild-mannered hero, Mr. Pupkin, is mistakenly thought to have confronted and chased off a burglar, he finds himself "exalted into the class of Napoleon Bonaparte and John Maynard and the Charge of the Light Brigade.")

Whatever its origins, Fontane's work became a textbook staple in such diverse parts of the globe as Russia, France, Hungary, Latvia, and even Korea. For many children in those countries, as for our German friend, the faraway *Eriesee* came to represent a place of adventure and peril, a fabulous sea of dreams that might or might not actually exist.

To the early French explorers, not only Lake Erie but the entire Great Lakes region appeared a bit fantastical, even overwhelming. Such huge bodies of water—were they lakes or oceans? So many wild animals never glimpsed in the dappled woods of Normandy and Brittany—what species were they? When these young noblemen, used to the domesticated countryside of northern France, got around to publishing accounts of their travels through the New World forests, their imaginations, and those of the illustrators, at times ran wild.

But the Frenchmen also admired what they saw. The Lake Erie shoreline, with its mild climate, its rich carpet of vegetation, its waterfowl-filled wetlands, and its waters as thick with fish as the Grand Banks, struck many of them as a kind of heaven on earth. Two young Sulpician priests, René de Bréhard de Gallinée and his friend Francis Dollier de Casson, couldn't stop raving about what they'd found on their 1669 voyage. (They are often cited as being the first Europeans to traverse the eastern part of the lake, although they were most likely preceded by fur trappers.)

When Benjamin Franklin visited Erie's south shore a century later, he was equally entranced by what he dubbed "the Mediterranean of the New World." A slick horse trader and a diehard Pennsylvanian, Franklin duped New York State into giving up a 50-mile stretch of prime waterfront for next to nothing, which is why today there is a port called Erie in the otherwise landlocked western portion of Franklin's home state. Over the next decades the lake played a significant part in the development of the North American continent. During the War of 1812, the boundary between the United States and Canada was decided once and for

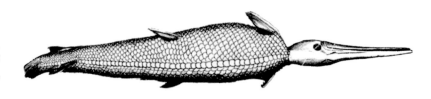

all by the armies and navies of Lake Erie; the last stand of the once-dominant Eastern Woodlands culture took place on its shores around the same time; and in 1825 the opening of the Erie Canal signaled the beginning of the first great wave of European immigration. Countless thousands of people were soon pouring off canal boats into the city of Buffalo, then embarking on passenger vessels that would carry them to Ohio's Western Reserve or the Michigan Territory or beyond. Always assuming, of course, that their vessel didn't meet the same fate as the fire-ravaged *Erie*.

Once the costly and divisive American Civil War came to an end in 1865, the late industrial revolution exploded along the lake. Budding industrialists had realized that the recently discovered oil and coal fields in western Pennsylvania, West Virginia and eastern Ohio could be combined with the vast iron-ore deposits of the upper lakes to create a new iron and steel industry. In what seemed like no time railroads, oil refineries, factories, foundries, power plants, shipyards and shipping terminals were springing up in Lake Erie ports, and the once tranquil American shoreline was changed forever.

Benjamin Franklin wasn't so far off when he described Erie as the Mediterranean of the New World. Like that other large, beautiful, multi-jurisdictional body of water, this lake has been affected by layer upon layer of history—Native families, explorers, soldiers of various armies, immigrants of every conceivable background and political outlook, preachers, hunters, fishers, industrialists, farmers, artists, naturalists, entertainers and fun-seekers have all left their mark.

There aren't many places on this continent with as many stories to tell.

Two of the creatures interpreted by artists in France from the explorer's descriptions. The huge gar pike, whose jaws measured about 3 feet, was depicted in the Jesuits' *Historia Canadensis*, published in the mid-seventeenth century. The stylishly coifed woolly buffalo is found in Louis Hennepin's 1697 Nouvelle découverte d'un très Grand Pays. *Historia Canadensis/Nouvelle decouverte d'un tres Grand Pays*

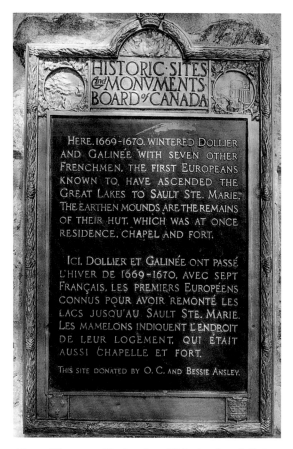

Here, 1669-1670, wintered Dollier and Galinée with seven other Frenchmen, the first Europeans known to have ascended the Great Lakes to Sault Ste. Marie. The earthen mounds are the remains of their hut, which was at once residence, chapel and fort.

Ici, Dollier et Galinée ont passé l'hiver de 1669-1670, avec sept Français, les premiers Européens connus pour avoir remonté les lacs jusqu'au Sault Ste. Marie. Les mamelons indiquent l'endroit de leur logement, qui était aussi chapelle et fort.

This site donated by O. C. and Bessie Ansley.

After paddling some 60 miles along Erie's shoreline, Gallinée and Dollier made camp for the winter of 1669–70 along a small river. In his diary, Galinée called their wintering place "the earthly paradise of Canada," and went on to exclaim, "The woods are open, crossed by rivers filled with fish and beavers . . . At one glance we saw more than 100 roebucks in a single herd . . . bears fatter and more flavourful than the most savory pigs of France." The glen in which they waited out the winter storms has been preserved by the citizens of Port Dover. The priests' winter hut is believed to have stood just behind the mounds in the foreground. *Corry Sobol*

The Erie Canal in 1894. Mules still towed the boats, as they always had. Just visible along the far shore is a more modern mode of transportation — an electric trolley car.
Historical Society of the Tonawandas

The *Empire*, a luxurious side-wheel lake steamer built in Cleveland in 1844, was renowned for its 230-foot dining salon, complete with orchestra. A typical passenger list included both poor immigrants and prosperous families on excursions. *A Pictorial History of the Great Lakes*

In Ashtabula Harbor, c. 1855–60, escaping slaves were hidden in the Hubbard & Co. warehouse in the mid-foreground. The midnight travelers would be smuggled aboard after dark, to be dropped off somewhere on the Canadian shore, depending on where the captain might have business. *Historical Collections of the Great Lakes, Bowling Green State University*

$200 Reward.

RANAWAY from the subscriber, on the night of Thursday, the 30th of Sepember,

FIVE NEGRO SLAVES,

To-wit: one Negro man, his wife, and three children.

The man is a black negro, full height, very erect, his face a little thin. He is about forty years of age, and calls himself *Washington Reed*, and is known by the name of Washington. He is probably well dressed, possibly takes with him an ivory headed cane, and is of good address. Several of his teeth are gone.

Mary, his wife, is about thirty years of age, a bright mulatto woman, and quite stout and strong.

The oldest of the children is a boy, of the name of FIELDING, twelve years of age, a dark mulatto, with heavy eyelids. He probably wore a new cloth cap.

MATILDA, the second child, is a girl, six years of age, rather a dark mulatto, but a bright and smart looking child.

MALCOLM, the youngest, is a boy, four years old, a lighter mulatto than the last, and about equally as bright. He probably also wore a cloth cap. If examined, he will be found to have a swelling at the navel.

Washington and Mary have lived at or near St. Louis, with the subscriber, for about 15 years.

It is supposed that they are making their way to Chicago, and that a white man accompanies them, that they will travel chiefly at night, and most probably in a covered wagon.

A reward of $150 will be paid for their apprehension, so that I can get them, if taken within one hundred miles of St. Louis, and $200 if taken beyond that, and secured so that I can get them, and other reasonable additional charges, if delivered to the subscriber, or to THOMAS ALLEN, Esq., at St. Louis. Mo. The above negroes, for the last few years, have been in possession of Thomas Allen, Esq., of St. Louis.

WM. RUSSELL.

ST. LOUIS, Oct. 1, 1847.

While Europeans headed westward in hopes of economic betterment, another sort of refugee was fleeing north to fulfill of an even more basic human desire — freedom from slavery. *Oberlin College Archives*

Downtown Buffalo, 1900. Of the United States' eight largest urban areas in 1920, one (Cleveland) lay midway along the lake, another (Detroit) on its western outlet, and a third (Buffalo) at the eastern end. Lively Buffalo was the smallest of the three, but justly celebrated for its coherent urban design and beautiful public buildings.
Library of Congress

Four Lake Erie region cronies: Henry Ford, Thomas Edison, President Warren Harding and rubber magnate Harvey Firestone, 1922. Ford hailed from Dearborn, near Detroit; Edison, the son of Canadians forced to flee across the lake after the failed Rebellion of 1837, was born a few miles west of Cleveland; Harding and Firestone were natives of farming villages just south of the lake.
Ohio Guide — WPA

The Welland Canal, at Port Colborne, Ontario, 1866. Lake Erie, which at the onset of the century was nearly empty of traffic, had grown into the world's busiest waterway by the time this picture was taken. That commercial triumph didn't stop the strict observance of the Sabbath in a still largely god-fearing society; the captains of these cargo carriers are impatiently waiting for the stroke of Sunday midnight, when the canal would reopen.
Port Colborne Historical and Marine Museum

By the end of the century, even smaller harbors such as this one in Tonawanda, New York, were overcrowded. *Historical Society of the Tonawandas*

Small-boat fishermen unloading their catch on a beach in Wheatley, near Leamington, 1926. Every visitor to the lake, from the earliest explorers on, had remarked on the amazing variety of delicious fish to be found there—whitefish, lake sturgeon, lake trout, herring, walleye, bass, perch, pike, sculpin. Poundnetters, who rigged their nets on posts set in shallow water; offshore seiners working out of dories; and fully-equipped fish tugs in the middle of the lake all staked out a place for themselves. By the time statistics began to be kept on such things, Lake Erie had become the world's largest freshwater fishery. *Courtesy of Dennis Jackson*

Harvesting tobacco on a Norfolk County farm, 1923. The mild Lake Erie climate lent itself to "southern" crops, and by the mid-1920s tobacco fields and orchards were everywhere on the north shore. "Tillsonburg, Tillsonburg, my back still hurts when I hear that word," goes the song by former picker Stompin' Tom Connors. *Archives of Ontario*

A 1920s camp meeting at Erie Beach Park, Fort Erie, Ontario. The lakeshore on both sides had become a popular setting for prayer meetings and mass baptisms. You could say that Erie is the most spiritual of the Great Lakes; it is the only one, perhaps the only lake anywhere, to boast its own gospel hymn. "Brightly Beams our Father's Mercy" (commonly known as "Let the Lower Lights Be Burning") climbed to the top of the Sunday school charts in the 1870s, and is still sung today. *Fort Erie Museum Board*

The long prayer services could be hard on children, so some resourceful person thought of putting up a small playground to keep them occupied. Then a carousel and perhaps a ride or two were added. Parents soon began casting envious eyes toward the fun their children were having. By the roaring twenties, religion had been relegated to a back seat and the one-time campgrounds had evolved into elaborate entertainment complexes that boasted huge ballrooms, gaudy amusement parks, midways, snack bars, casinos and sports stadiums—all fronted by wide sandy beaches. The famous Racer, one of the first of the modern roller coasters, opened for business at Cedar Point, Ohio, in 1910. *Cedar Point Historical Archives*

Angler · Port Dover Oct 1907

The collision of Arctic fronts pushing down from northern Canada with subtropical highs pressing up from the south can result in sudden storms with powerful, compact waves. When gale force winds appear from nowhere, all a sailor can do is run for home, as the captain of the Port Dover fish tug *Angler* is doing in this 1907 photo. *Authors' Collection*

Thousands of wrecks, ranging from early two-man bateaux (flat-bottomed, double-headed rowboats with a single square sail) to once-elegant steamers and huge ore carriers, lie spread out on the lake's sandy bottom, a grim testimony to what can transpire in a sudden Lake Erie storm. *Courtesy of Rob Cromwell*

Taking advantage of the timeless bounty of the lake, a family gathers driftwood near Port Dover, 1910. *AO*

The shoreline at Long Point. Despite all the fevered human activity, certain parts of Lake Erie's shoreline remained virtually untouched. In the western basin, Point Pelee early on became a prime site for ecological research, as well as the birding mecca of the Midwest. And toward the eastern end of the lake, opposite Erie, Pennsylvania, lies Long Point, second in significance only to Chesapeake Bay as a North American wetlands. Preserved by a combination of good luck and rare nineteenth-century ecological foresight, the world's longest freshwater sand spit stayed pretty much as nature made it and today is protected as a World Biosphere Reserve. *AO*

Chapter One

PREHISTORY TO 1783

The prehistory of Lake Erie and the entire Great Lakes region is a story that geologists and archaeologists continually revise. One point they do agree on is that an ancient river system, formed unfathomable eons ago by the normal processes of wind and water, predates the Ice Ages. When the glaciers arrived some two million years ago, they gouged their way south across Canada and far down into present-day Ohio. The first of them widened the existing river valleys into lakes, and then each succeeding retreat and resurgence of the ice reshaped the lakes' terrain into a new configuration. The series of lake ridges overlooking the New York and Pennsylvania shorelines are remnants of earlier lacustrine incarnations.

When the last of the glaciers finally retreated some twelve thousand years ago, the landscape they left behind looked not much

An arrowhead pendant, c. A.D. 1000, found at Long Point, Ontario. *Courtesy of Archaeological Services, Inc.*

The rebounding land cut off the Ottawa River outlet, causing water to spill southward and creating a new drainage system through Lake Ontario and the St. Lawrence River. Research suggests that within the space of a few years, not even a blink of the eye geologically speaking, water levels in the lower lakes rose as much as 45 feet. That may be a bit too abrupt, but in any event the transition was rapid. Whole forests and Native settlements, perhaps whole civilizations, vanished forever. At Erie's eastern end, the cataclysmic flood also created (or rather recreated, since in one of the lake's earlier incarnations a waterfall had already existed there) what would become the honeymoon haven of Niagara Falls. Unfortunately for the future of wedding planners, scientists predict that before another millennium passes the falls will crumble into a mere rapids. *AO*

different from the present-day Great Lakes basin, except that the upper lakes drained east through a channel roughly approximating the Ottawa River. At this time Lake Erie, too far south to be part of the system, was a smallish, landlocked body of water, cut off from her sister lakes. Then around 3400 B.C., a phenomenon known as isostatic rebound changed everything. The earth, liberated by the melting of the glacier from the weight of ice up to a mile thick,

The 17-foot grooves in this rock formation on Kelleys Island, an American island in the lake's western basin, demonstrate the gouging power of the glaciers' teeth-like edges. Before the island was quarried for its limestone, the rock formation extended 2,000 feet and was 17 feet in depth. *Courtesy of Follet House/Sandusky Library*

slowly began to rise, the way a sponge does after a hand that has been pressing down heavily is suddenly lifted.

As the glacier retreated, our prehistoric ancestors arrived. Contemporary archaeologists estimate that close to half a million bits and pieces of artifacts have been retrieved in recent years. The most spectacular finds have been at Fort Erie, Ontario, in the shadow of the Peace Bridge. As far back as 1764, when the original fort was being erected at the entrance to the Niagara River, workmen recorded finding strange-looking stone tools. When settlers arrived a few decades later, they frequently turned up human bones and flint fragments while digging their vegetable gardens. So it's no surprise to learn that by the late nineteenth century amateur archaeologists were hard at work on the spot, speculating that the entire area was the site of some sort of significant prehistoric activity. However, it wasn't until the early 1980s, when one cache of bones was judged to belong to American soldiers killed in the War of 1812, that large-scale excavation began, courtesy of the U.S. Army's bottomless pockets. One fine day in 1985, a team was scraping away at the wall of a grave when three prehistoric flint tools fell out. When a bit more digging uncovered additional artifacts, someone finally asked Ron Williamson, who was overseeing the dig, how old he thought all these things might be. "About four thousand years," he replied casually. He was almost dead on; the team had stumbled on an ancient flint factory dating back to at least the beginning of the third millennium B.C.

North American archeologists had long been aware that a vast trading network encompassing the Mississippi and Great Lakes' basins and beyond had existed between approximately 800 B.C. and A.D. 1250. Copper from Lake Superior, silver and cobalt from northern Ontario, galena from Quebec, shell and shark's teeth and alligator skulls from the Gulf of Mexico and the Atlantic, metal artifacts from the mound-building cultures of the Midwest, hematite from Michigan, obsidian from the Black Hills and the Rockies and mica from the Appalachians made their way up and down the continent's rivers. The spectacular Fort Erie revelations added yet one more piece to the archeological jigsaw puzzle.

On May 19, 1535, Jacques Cartier sailed from the French port of St. Malo on his second voyage to the New World. He was searching for the fabled passage to China and its legendary treasures, but fifty days later found himself in the Gulf of St. Lawrence instead. He continued on up the great river all the way to the future Île de Montréal, where he planted a cross and claimed the land for the French Crown. Soon afterwards, possibly for reasons related to the coming of the Europeans, the nations of southern Ontario undertook a major geographic consolidation: the Hurons resettled east of Georgian Bay, the Tobacco and Petun around the Bruce Peninsula, and the Neutrals between the Niagara and Grand Rivers. And a tribe known as the Erie or Eriege became active around the southeastern end of their namesake lake, in present-day New York and Pennsylvania.

Though the precious metals they sought proved elusive, the treasure seekers soon hit on a resource almost equally valuable — a ubiquitous, thick-bodied rodent with a glossy coat that served extremely well for protection from rain and cold. When fashionable Europe went mad for beaver coats, hats, muffs, and anything else made from the creature's silky fur, Native trappers brought in pelts by the millions to barter for iron tools and decorative items. Along with these, unfortunately, came less desirable legacies like smallpox and liquor.

The Iroquois of upstate New York played a key role both as trappers and as contacts between the whites and the tribes along the upper Great Lakes. In the process they grew increasingly rich and powerful; however, when the easily accessible supply of beaver in their territory ran out and the western tribes began to wonder why they needed middlemen, the Iroquois were left with no product to barter. Seeing their new lifestyle about to disappear, they decided to eliminate the competition. Crossing Lake Ontario in 1648, a coalition of Five Nations forces (they wouldn't become Six Nations until 1722, when the Tuscarora officially joined the confederation) drove north to attack the Huron, and gradually eliminated them as a cohesive civilization. In ensuing years they moved west and then south, methodically eradicating the

An aerial view of Elgin County. Repeated advances and retreats of the heavy ice sheets flattened out the landscape. That's particularly true in southwestern Ontario, where long stretches look so flat you feel that if you laid down a carpenter's level anywhere at random the little bubble would stay squarely in the middle. *Parks Canada/Fort Malden National Historic Site*

Tobacco, Petun, and Neutral peoples. Finally, they headed back across the lake to wipe out the Erie and their close relations, the Delaware. Earlier smallpox epidemics may explain the ease with which these once-powerful nations were destroyed; the Neutrals, for example, are estimated to have lost a third of their population in the outbreak of 1638.

In 1760, the French surrendered control of the entire northeastern half of North America after being defeated in a conflict known to the American colonialists as the French and Indian War, and to European historians as the Seven Year's War. The relatively laissez-faire French attitude toward Native nations was replaced by the more disdainful approach of the British. A Native coalition, led by the Ottawa chief Pontiac, rose up against the harsh rule of Commander-in-Chief Lord Jeffrey Amherst and torched British forts from Wisconsin to Western Pennsylvania.

Numerous small homesteads were burned as well. Two thousand white settlers, mostly in western Pennsylvania and eastern Ohio, perished in the summer of 1763.

No sooner had the Natives been suppressed than a different sort of agitation began to build along the eastern seaboard. The colonialists, many of them by now third- and fourth-generation Americans, were suddenly demanding the right to run their own affairs. "On the 18th of April in '75," so the Longfellow poem goes, a mere sixteen years after Wolfe and Montcalm had died on the Plains of Abraham and control of North America had fallen into British hands, Paul Revere set off on his celebrated midnight ride. One year later the newly formed United States of America declared its independence, and six years after that, to the surprise of the world and possibly the colonialists themselves, the proud British army was sent scurrying back to Europe.

The shocking rapidity with which the United States had come into existence left many jurisdictional questions unanswered, particularly concerning ownership of the vast areas around the Great Lakes. It would take another war, fought mainly on and around Lake Erie, to settle the boundaries.

In 1899, David Boyle, popularly known as the father of Canadian archeology, excavated human burial mounds on Pelee Island. The mounds have subsequently been dated to 100–400 B.C. Since Doyle's day, a wide range of old material has turned up near the Ontario shore, including fifteenth-century pottery and other ceramics at Catfish Creek near Aylmer and a thousand-year-old human skeleton and burial goods carbon dated to 900–700 B.C., both at Long Point. The discovery of truly ancient (9000 B.C.) spear points near London provided clear evidence that not long after the ice retreated for good, primitive hunters were roaming the lakeside tundra in search of caribou and mastodon. *AO*

Projectile points shown here date from the Genessee period, 2000–1500 B.C. Fort Erie was built on an extensive bed of chert, a form of flint that is easily worked and produces particularly hard, keen edges. *ASI*

A seventeenth-century thunderbird gorget measuring about 1.5 by 2.5 inches. During one dig, five thousand artifacts, ranging from late Archaic (3000–1000 B.C.) to late Iroquoian (A.D. 900–1650) were found in a single cubic yard of earth. *ASI*

Around A.D. 1400, the intracontinental trading network went into an unexplained decline and the lower lakes came to be dominated by a series of Iroquoian peoples: to the east by the five nations of the Iroquois Confederacy; to the north and west by the Huron and their shadowy relatives, the Tobacco, Petun and Neutrals. This reconstruction of a Neutral longhouse depicts a scene that would have been typical of any of these culturally interrelated nations. *ASI*

According to an 1896 Pennsylvania atlas, many farmers along the South shore reported finding ancient mounds and earthworks on their properties. Across the lake, these low earthworks, near Port Stanley, Ontario, marked the outer edge of a palisaded Neutral settlement of approximately eight hundred people. It was abandoned around A.D. 1500. Exactly who the Neutrals were, what language they spoke, and how they organized their nation is still something of a mystery. We don't even know what they called themselves—the name by which we refer to them today was assigned by Samuel de Champlain, who mistakenly thought them to be pacifists. *Corry Sobol*

Iroquoian rock carvings are common throughout the Great Lakes area. One of the finest examples along Lake Erie is Inscription Rock, a giant boulder located on Kelleys Island on the American side. Time and tourism have unfortunately worn away some of the drawings, but depictions of clothing, snowshoes, serpents, war clubs and sacred objects shed light on ceremonial and everyday life among the people who once lived here. *FH/SL*

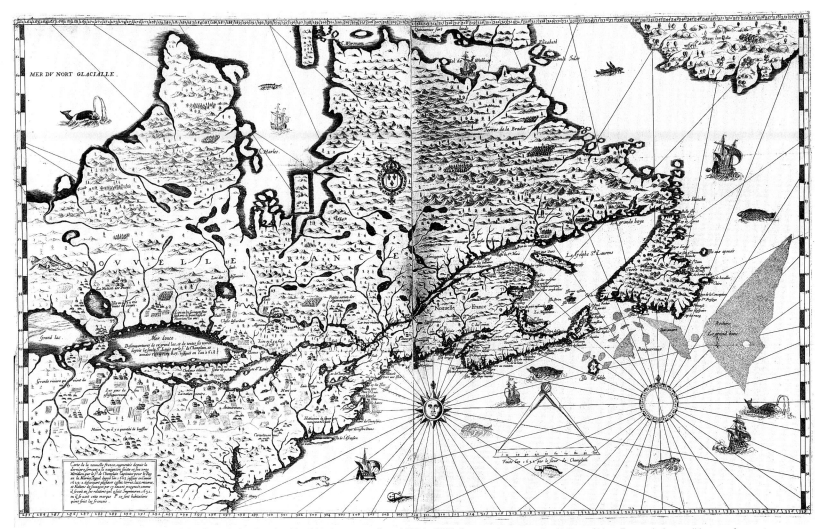

Champlain pioneered the exploration of the Great Lakes interior. For thirty-two years, from 1603 to 1635, the man known as the Father of New France led expeditions as far west as Georgian Bay and southwestern Ontario and south into present-day New York State. His memorial is not found in a portrait (none exists), but in the impressive collection of maps and reports he sent back to France. This 1632 map provided the first complete, although not especially accurate, depiction of the chain of lakes in the little-known region beyond the St. Lawrence. Lakes Erie and Ontario are mere blips beneath a large body of water marked as *Mer Douce* (Lake Huron). *National Archives of Canada*

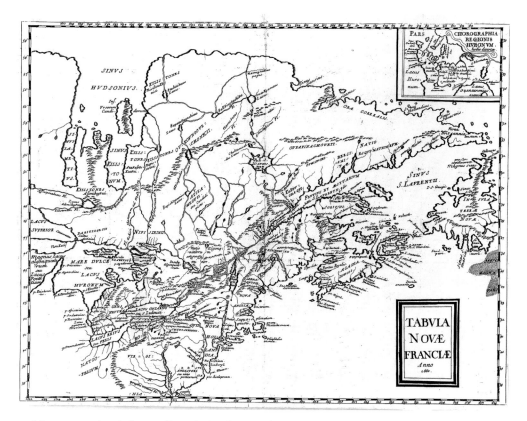

Other cartographers built upon Champlain's efforts, and by 1660 François du Creux had traced the geography of the lakes with relative clarity. On his map, as on Champlain's, Erie is designated Lac du Chat or Felis. Wildcats were common along the lakeshore in those days, and Erie is thought to mean "large cat." *NAC*

Beaver remained the fur of choice in Europe for over 300 years, as these fashionable turn-of-the-nineteenth-century hats demonstrate. *Hudson's Bay Company Archives*

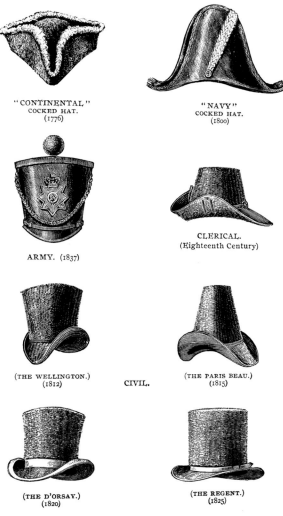

"CONTINENTAL"
COCKED HAT.
(1776)

"NAVY"
COCKED HAT.
(1800)

ARMY. (1837)

CLERICAL.
(Eighteenth Century)

(THE WELLINGTON.)
(1812)

CIVIL.

(THE PARIS BEAU.)
(1815)

(THE D'ORSAY.)
(1820)

(THE REGENT.)
(1825)

MODIFICATIONS OF THE BEAVER HAT.

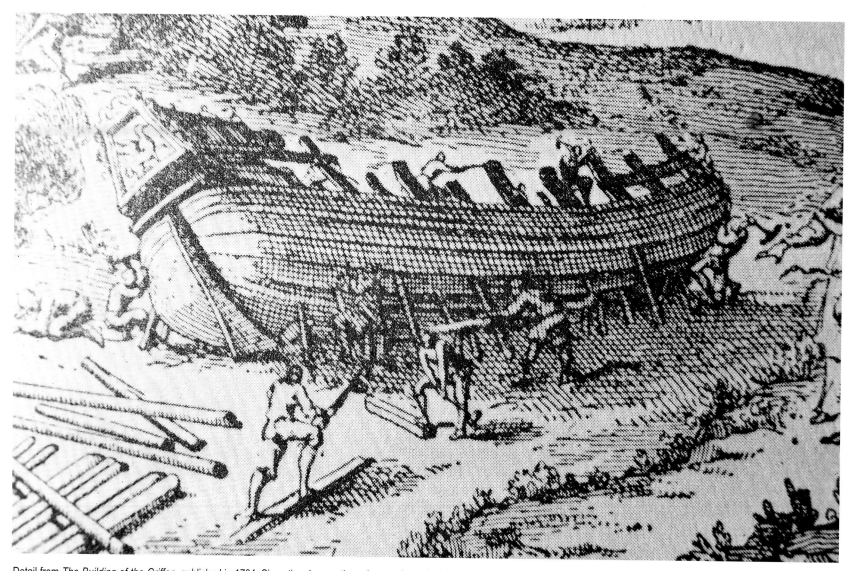

Detail from *The Building of the Griffon*, published in 1704. Since time began, the only vessels on the lake had been canoes. That changed in 1679 when the over-ambitious Chevalier de la Salle built the *Griffon* at Cuyaga Creek, a tributary of the Niagara River. When the 60-foot barque was launched on August 7, it became the first sailing vessel to ply Erie and the upper lakes. After nearly foundering off Long Point, the ship continued on through Lake Huron to the shores of Lake Michigan, where it loaded up with beaver pelts and started back. It was never seen again, which makes the *Griffon* not only the first ship to sail the upper lakes, but the first to be lost on them. La Salle was not aboard on the fateful trip; he lived long enough to make a pioneering voyage down the Mississippi to the Gulf Coast, where he was murdered by disenchanted crewmen in 1687. *Parks Canada/Point Pelee National Park*

Fort Pontchartrain, 1705. In the late seventeenth century, the once empty shores of Lake Erie began to fill in. Fortified trading posts were built by the French on the Niagara River as early as 1679 and at Fort Pontchartrain (Detroit) in 1701. Later they erected a string of forts extending from the sandy peninsula of Presque Isle (Erie, Pennsylvania) down to the site of present-day Pittsburgh, and the British replied by putting up some of their own farther west. At the same time, Native nations from Indiana and Illinois were migrating into the Ohio region and, as the eighteenth century wore on, a small vanguard of hardy British homesteaders pushed into the region from the other direction.
Courtesy of U.S. Army Signal Corps.

After Amherst was replaced, Pontiac made peace with the British, who awarded their new ally a commemorative medal. The award did him more harm than good, since his new stance angered many of the younger warriors. He and his family were driven off their land, and in 1769, Pontiac was assassinated. *AO*

35

NOTICE is hereby given by the General Agent for the Payment of Militia Provincial Pensions, pursuant to the directions contained in the Seventh Section of the Militia Pensions Act, passed in the last Session of the Legislature, that having received the Sum of Six Thousand Five Hundred Pounds, for the purpose of paying the said Pensions for the period up to the 31st of December next; the same are now in Course of Payment.

LIST of disabled Persons who have heretofore been admitted, and of those also who Claim to be admitted, as Militia Pensioners this Province, on account of the Wounds received in Action, or Disability occasioned by Casualties or Accidents, which have occurred on Actual Service in defence of the Province, as far as Returns have been received; with the sums due to those who produced the necessary Certificates and Documents to touching their Wounds and Disability; and which will be due to others have produced those Documents in part, when they will have furnished them complete as required by Law, up to the 31st of December, 1816.

Name of Pensioner	Rank	Regiment or Description of Service to which belonged	Action or Place where wounded, &c.	Time when Wounded	Period for which Pension is due From	To	Amount of Pens Province Curr' Dollars at 5s £.	S.	D
Titus G. Simons	Major	2d York, now 1st Gore	Lundy's Lane	25 July 1814	1 Jan. 1815	31 Dec. 1815	20		
James Kirby	Major	2d Lincoln and In. Militia	Fort Erie & Lundy's Lane	2 Dec. 1812 & 25 July 1814	2 Dec. 1812	do do	81	12	10.
William Jarvie	Captain	Incorporated	York	27 Apr. 1813	1 Jan. 1815	do do	40		
John McDonell	do	do	Lundy's Lane	25 July 1814	1 Jan. 1816	do do	20		
Thomas Fraser	do	do	do	do do	25 July 1814	do do	48	15	4
John McGregor	do	Kent Volunteers	Long Woods	4 Mar. 1814	1 Jan. 1816	do do	20		
Philip Empey	Lieutenant	1st Stormont	Ogdensburgh	22 Feb. 1813	do	do do	20		
Thomas Smith	do	Late 2nd York	Lundy's Lane	25 July 1814	13 Nov. 1815	do do	22	2	8.
Henry Ruttan	do	Incorporated	do	do	1 Jan. 1816	do do	20		
George Ryerson	do	1st Norfolk	Fort Erie	28 Nov. 1812	do	do do	20		
ames McGregor	do	Kent Volunteers	River Thames	9 July 1814	9 July 1814	do do	49	12	3.
Daniel McDougal	do	Incorporated	Lundy's Lane	25 July 1814	25 July do	do do	48	15	4
Robert Kirkpatrick	Ensign	2nd Lincoln	Chippawa	5 July 1814	5 do	do do	49	15	7.
Donald McDearmid	Lieutenant	1st Glengary	Ogdensburgh	22 Feb. 1813	22 Feb. 1813	do do	77	1	4.
James Richardson	Master's Mate	Provincial Marine	Oswego	6 May 1814	6 May 1814	do do	53	3	

Chapter Two

WAR COMES TO THE LAKE

After the Revolutionary War, several eastern states laid claims to large portions of the Ohio Territory. They backed their demands by citing old royal charters, blithely overlooking the fact that they had just fought a war to free themselves from monarchical authority. Under pressure from Congress, the states reluctantly agreed to cede portions of their claims over to veterans. In mid-northern Ohio, for example, 100 acres were offered to a noncom, 150 to an ensign, 200 to a lieutenant and 1,100 to a major general. Virginia, which claimed most of southern and central Ohio, was even more generous, awarding up to 15,000 acres, depending on rank. An area of 500,000 acres along the lake, known as the Sufferers' Lands, was set aside to compensate Connecticut citizens whose homes had been torched by the British army. (In the end the federal government would brush aside all these assertions of possession, and the western territories would be divided into new states.)

By the early 1790s, an estimated twenty thousand men, women and children a year were making their way over the Appalachians to Fort Pitt (Pittsburgh), the gateway to the territories. Here, the

Left: Pension lists, published after the War of 1812, recording those eligible for compensation from the British government. The high proportion of men wounded in battles on or near Lake Erie illustrates the region's pivotal role. *Simcoe Public Library*

"Mad Anthony" Wayne, 1791, painting by James Herring. *Metro Toronto Reference Library*

The Great Black Swamp, a disease-ridden 5,000-thousand-square-mile bog, extended all the way from present day Vermilion to the current Indiana border. Geologically, the swamp was a relic of the last ice age, an unstable lowland still resettling after the melting of the glacier and the resulting isostatic rebound. This contemporary picture, taken at Old Woman Creek State Park, near Huron, Ohio, one of the few remaining patches of original marshland, gives a sense of how forbidding the landscape must have appeared to settlers. *CS*

great majority crowded onto flatboats and set off on a leisurely voyage down the Ohio River toward that long-dreamt-of piece of farmland in one of the territories bordering the river. Only a few brave souls opted to veer north through the towering, densely packed oak and maple savannah toward Lake Erie, and those who did found every step a struggle. For one thing there were as yet no roads, not even a trail wide enough on which to drive a team of oxen. And the further west you traveled, the worse it got.

Barely penetrable forest, mosquitoes the size of dragonflies and rising swamp fever were bad enough, but even more menacing was the ever-present threat of attack from "savages." Iroquois warriors, angry about being driven from their traditional lands in upstate New York; Huron and Ottawa who had once lived north of the lake; Shawnee from Kentucky; Miami, Kickapoo, Delaware, Ojibwa, and Potawatamie drifting into the area from the Michigan and Indiana territories; even Winnebago, Illinois, Sauk and Fox raiding parties from as far away as the Mississippi River were all primed for a showdown with the land-hungry newcomers. Roving bands of warriors began slaughtering settlers in the Ohio country by the hundreds and destroying their newly cultivated farms.

In 1790, President Washington responded to the settlers' anguished pleas for help by sending in troops, commanded by General Josiah Harmar. The old soldier had been a Revolutionary War hero, but he was no match for the coalition put together by the redoubtable Miami Chief, Little Turtle. After enticing Harmer deep into their territory, the Natives sprang a trap along the Maumee River and cut his army to pieces. When another old-timer, General Arthur St. Clair, suffered an even more devastating defeat, Washington handed command to a man he could count on to make good use of his advantage in arms and numbers—General Anthony Wayne.

In August of 1794, at the Battle of Fallen Timbers near present-day Toledo, Wayne's well-drilled troops destroyed the Native armies. Then the general, nicknamed "Mad Anthony" for his fiery disposition, went on to "teach them a lesson" by torching every Native village he could find. One Native warrior did learn from the

United Empire Loyalist refugees arriving at their new home. The wilds of the Great Lakes were a far cry from the comfortable environs they had been used to on the American east coast. *James Peachy is the artist.*

defeats, though not in quite the way Wayne had anticipated. He was a hereditary Shawnee chief by the name of Tecumseh, and the long hours he spent studying the white man's tactics would later help him become perhaps the greatest of all Native commanders.

With the threat of Native attacks lessened, small communities began springing up on the American shoreline. Between 1796 and 1810, the villages of Buffalo, Cleveland, Erie, Ashtabula, Lorain and Conneaut were founded; streets were laid out; and schools, churches and town halls erected. In 1803, Ohio celebrated its new statehood, and after the marshy landscape at the lake's western curve was drained, the new settlements of Toledo and Sandusky were added.

Back east, citizens who had chosen to remain faithful to the Crown during the war were finding life difficult. In some districts "Tories" were barred from voting, and in other places they were stripped of their land or run out of town on a rail by angry mobs. In the face of such strong hostility, thousands opted to pack up and head north to Canada, where they would become known as United Empire Loyalists, or UELs. Most settled in Lower Canada (Quebec) and the Maritimes, but by the early 1800s a substantial number were taking up the tempting offer of free land in Upper Canada (Ontario). Loyalist heads of families could claim 100 acres, single men received 50 acres, NCOs 200, and on up for the upper ranks. The grants continued into the second generation, when sons were eligible for 200 acres when they reached maturity and daughters 200 at marriage.

For many immigrants, their new lives represented all they could hope for. "It is a pretty thing to stand at one's own door and see a hundred acres of land of his own," as one settler put it in a letter back home. On the other hand, in these North American woods you had to be on the lookout for dangers unknown for many years in most of the old world—hungry bears, for instance. William Pope, one of many talented artist-soldiers in the British Army, sketched this Norfolk County scene in the early 1830s. *Norfolk Historical Society/Eva Brook Donly Museum*

The Edison family of New Jersey were typical UEL settlers. Royalist to the core, they had headed north as soon as the 1783 Treaty of Paris confirmed the British defeat; after spending two decades in Nova Scotia, this large extended family, then numbering twenty, purchased a farm outside Port Burwell. There they joined with other newly arrived UEL families to provide leadership in the fledgling community, a pattern repeated in other settlements along the lake. British immigrants had also begun to trickle into the area, as had a large number of non-UEL Americans. In fact, some historians estimate that between 1795 and 1812 there were more of these former Yankees than British and Canadians combined looking for land in Upper Canada.

These American immigrants were not as casual as it might seem about giving up their citizenship. As they saw it, they would soon be Yankees again, when the region, not to mention the rest of Canada, was absorbed by the United States. Invasion of Canada had been a rebel priority during the Revolutionary War, and though early attempts failed, Washington was still mulling over another try right up to the end of the war. Both Benjamin Franklin and John Adams at different times drew up plans for occupying Canada, and Thomas Jefferson never ceased to believe that the manifest destiny of America was to control the entire continent. (Conquering Canada would require "merely a march," he commented dismissively when someone brought up the possibility of Canadian resistance.) And after the founding fathers had left the Washington scene, the two most powerful politicians in the country, Henry Clay and John Calhoun, once more took up the cry for conquest of the north.

It didn't take a Nostradamus to predict trouble ahead for the region.

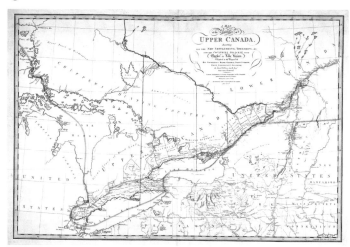

Map of Upper Canada, 1800. John Graves Simcoe, lieutenant governor of Upper Canada in the 1790s, became concerned about all the cross-border settlers. One of his strategies to stem the tide was the publication of this definitive map of Upper Canada, so there would be no doubt in anyone's mind who owned what. *AO*

The War of 1812

Eventually the United States declared war, citing Britain's high-handed regulation of ocean-going trade and insistence on searching U.S. vessels for crew with British citizenship. The Americans had also been goaded by what they saw as too cozy a relationship between the British and the Natives. And the fact that Tecumseh had been made a colonel in the redcoat army seemed to prove that they were encouraging the Native forces to go on the warpath again. But these issues, while aggravating, were really minor problems. The essential sticking point was ownership of the vast territories bordering the Great Lakes. The War of 1812, most historians agree, was fundamentally a war over land.

On paper, the United States held all the cards. Its population of six million was twelve times greater than Canada's; the population was also less spread out and therefore, at least in theory, easier to mobilize. Besides, the mother country's life-and-death struggle with Napoleon for dominance in Europe was reaching a climax, leaving the North American military cupboard nearly bare. The total of British troops on hand to defend all of Canada came to less than nine thousand. A little daring and imagination and the colony would be conquered before the toffee noses and macaronies in London even realized the war was on. Or so the Americans assumed.

From the start, the War of 1812 was a disorganized, out-of-kilter conflict, full of confused strategies and personal jealousies. Before the first shots were fired, a volley of posters and broadsheets was sent into Upper Canada to notify the citizenry of the coming opportunity to be "emancipated from British tyranny" and "restored to the dignified station of freemen." However, such high-principled offers failed to entice Canadians, and although some of the recently arrived cross-border settlers joined the U.S. forces, most UEL families thought back to their treatment after the Revolutionary War and hurried off to join Canadian militias instead.

Conducting a war in a distant, unfamiliar tract of forest and swamp promised challenges in supply and communications, and early on it became clear that leadership in the field would be the critical element—a resourceful commander would win battles, an inept one would lose them. As it happened, both sides were well supplied with each type. One of President Madison's first official decisions after war was declared was to follow Washington's lead and appoint a Revolutionary War hero to command the western armies, and, like Washington, Madison came to regret his choice. General William Hull, the governor of the Michigan Territory, had led a heroic bayonet charge at the Battle of Stony Point back in 1778, under the command of Anthony Wayne. But thirty-four years is a long time, and the once-gallant soldier had long since forgotten the art of warfare.

Hull started out well, landing his troops on July 12, 1812, at Sandwich (Windsor) without encountering resistance. But even though his men greatly outnumbered the small garrison at Fort Malden, instead of pressing on the 20 miles to attack that fort, he opted to make camp and wait for the reinforcements he had requisitioned from Ohio. The delay gave Tecumseh a chance to gather his men, and when the Ohioans finally showed up south of Detroit he was waiting in ambush. The militiamen were sent fleeing back to their home state. When a second American column met the same fate, the shaken Hull pulled his army back across the river.

Three Grand River veterans of the War of 1812. This picture of elders Jacob Warner, John Tutlee and John Smoke Johnson, taken in 1886 when the men were in their nineties, is a reminder that many Iroquois were among the families who resettled in Canada after the American Revolution. Like the United Empire Loyalists, they had been given land grants, notably along the Grand River, and when the War of 1812 broke out many fought alongside (and often ahead of) the British regulars and Canadian militias. *Woodland Cultural Center*

One factor the Americans failed to consider was the genius of Tecumseh. He seems to have inspired deep respect, both as a political leader and a military man, in everyone he met. Even William Henry Harrison, a hero of the Indian wars and one of Tecumseh's deadliest enemies, described him as "one of those uncommon geniuses which spring up occasionally to produce revolutions and overturn the established order of things." The British colonel's uniform in this painting by Benson John Lossing is accurate enough, and the single eagle feather is a nice touch, but the strangely effete look is exceedingly unlikely. Unfortunately, no contemporary portrait of the great chief is known to exist. *MTRL*

On the other side of the Atlantic, the populace of England was not all that keen about taking on another obscure and expensive war. This London cartoon, in which John Bull is seen baking a new batch of "ships for the lakes," expresses some of these doubts. "Here are more Guns for the Lake service. If ever they do but get there—I hear the last you sent were waylaid by a sly Yankee fox," says one of the bakers. *MTRL*

A British light infantry officer.

A trooper of the British 19th Light Dragoons.
The British may not have won all their battles,
but you couldn't beat them for fancy dress.
Parks Canada/Fort Malden Historical Site

Hull chose the frontier town of Detroit as the jumping off point for an invasion of Upper Canada. His strategy was to cross the Detroit River, taking the enemy by surprise, then move on to capture Fort Malden (Amherstburg) and nearby Bois Blanc (Boblo) Island. That would give him control of the entrance to Lake Erie; from there, Hull planned to march east and link up with a second force approaching from Niagara. Together, they would lay waste to southwestern Ontario. After a promising start, he lost his nerve and quickly retreated to his starting place. The blockhouse, abandoned after the war and shown here in 1903, was a key element in the island's defenses. *LC*

On August 13, 1812, the charismatic, battle-hardened Sir Isaac Brock arrived with new troops. Unlike his opponent, Brock intended to force the issue. Together with Tecumseh, he worked out a plan for the invasion of Detroit. (The two men hit it off immediately. "*This* is a man," Tecumseh is reported to have commented after their initial conversation.) Their strategy included a bombardment from the Canadian side that so intimidated the American commander that, to the fury of his officers, he surrendered the fort with hardly a return shot fired. Enthused by this easy victory, Native armies under Tecumseh's impassioned leadership rampaged through the Midwest, overrunning several key American frontier forts. *AO*

The Battle of Queenston Heights. After taking Detroit, Brock hurried east to deal with a new American invasion, but now it was the turn of the British to meet with disaster. In one of the last battles before winter set in, at Queenston Heights above the Niagara River, the regular army troops, Canadian militia and Iroquois together fought off the invaders. In the process, however, Brock was killed. The British never found another commander approaching his ability; if he had lived, the outcome of the war and the entire geopolitical balance of North America might have been quite different. *MTRL*

The defense of Fort Stephenson, 1813. Even though Brock was gone, Tecumseh's Native army was still prepared to fight. In July of 1813, a combined British and Native force attacked Fort Stephenson, located just south of Sandusky, but this time they came a cropper. The Americans, under the command of twenty-one-year-old Major George Croghan, although greatly outnumbered and with only a single cannon, held off the enemy in charge after charge until they finally broke and fled the field. Croghan became a national hero. And Tecumseh rightly began to question the abilities of General Henry Proctor, the man who had taken Brock's place. *Brown University Library*

On the American side, Hull had been removed from command and court martialed. To succeed him, President Madison appointed a pair of ambitious young turks, William Henry Harrison (above) and Winfield Scott. They spent the summer of 1813 repelling British and Native attacks, then seized the initiative. In October, in the Battle of Moraviantown, near Chatham, Harrison crushed the enemy forces under the plodding Proctor and brought southwestern Ontario under American control. An additional catastrophe for the redcoats was the death in battle of the inspirational Tecumseh. With their leader gone, the Native coalition quickly dispersed. *Erie County Historical Society, steel engraving by Edwin Williams*

The events of 1812 had brought home to the Americans the importance of gaining control of Lake Erie to ensure free shipment of supplies and communications. For the task of clearing the British navy off the lake, the American navy chose a young captain by the name of Oliver Hazard Perry. It was a tall order for a young man of twenty-eight whose battle experience was limited to the Barbary Coast skirmishes of a few years earlier. Undaunted, Perry spent the summer of 1813 building his fleet in the protected harbor of Erie, Pennsylvania, and no doubt wondering at times what he would do if the Royal Navy sent in raiding parties before his new fleet had even left the ways. Fortunately for him, the British had turned command of their lake fleet over to an even younger and equally untested man; at twenty-six, Robert Barclay could claim thirteen years of sea warfare under his belt, but none as commander of a squadron, or even of a single vessel. While Barclay spent the summer aimlessly patrolling the lake, Perry completed his fleet and sailed it safely out of harbor.
Lake Erie Islands Historical Society

The two evenly matched fleets met on September 12 off Put-in-Bay Island. The British captain may have been an inexperienced tactician, but he was no coward and his men fought tenaciously. Perry's unbending will, however, carried his men through. When the American's flagship, the *Lawrence*, was shattered under his feet by cannon fire, he had himself rowed to the *Niagara*, where he continued the fight with increased fury. (Left to right: the *Lady Prevost*, the *Chippeway*, the *Little Belt*, the *Niagara*, the *Queen Charlotte*, the *Detroit*, the *Scorpion*, the *Ariel*, the *General Hunter*, the *Trippe*, the *Caledonia*, the *Porcupine*, the *Tigress*, the *Somers*, and the *Lawrence*.) After the British colors were finally lowered, he sent his famous victory message: "We have met the enemy and they are ours." And so was Lake Erie. Barkley, like Hull, was court martialed after the defeat. *MTRL, Perry's Victory Peace Memorial*

That the British and Canadian forces did not lose all the battles of 1813 is due, in part, to the thirty-eight-year-old wife of a Loyalist militia officer. At Queenston, in the Niagara Peninsula, Laura Second overheard American officers planning a surprise attack on Lieutenant James FitzGibbon's outpost at Beaver Dams. Setting out on a daunting 30-mile trek through the American lines, she arrived just in time for the lieutenant to send out a detachment of Caugnawaga. The warriors ambushed the Yanks and so intimidated them that the entire force of five hundred men surrendered. Today she is as well known for the chocolates that bear her name as for her heroism. When the candy company was founded in 1913, the only available photograph was one of her in her old age, and a drawing taken from it that became part of the company's logo. Over time, her image miraculously grew younger, until she evolved backwards into today's rosy-cheeked, smiling young girl in a décolleté neckline. *Laura Secord Archives*

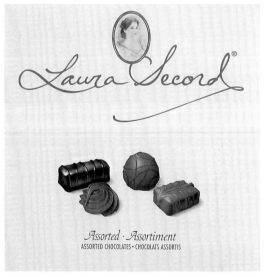

48

In May 1814, in retaliation for the mid-winter torching of Buffalo, an American force landed near Port Dover and burned that village to the ground. The raiders then rampaged along the shoreline, destroying mills, distilleries, public buildings and private residences. One eyewitness claimed that in the 20-mile stretch between Port Dover and Turkey Point hardly a house was left standing. It took years for the area to recover. Backus Mill, built in 1795 near Port Rowan, was one of the few important structures to survive. Today, it still grinds out flour, but for the edification of tourists. *Long Point Conservation Authority*

The Battle of Lundy's Lane, as depicted by C. W. Jeffreys. In a summer of bitter, bloody battles, one of the fiercest was fought on July 25, 1814, almost within sight of Niagara Falls. It ended with the British and Canadians driving the Americans back toward Fort Erie. By the end of August, the two exhausted armies had retired to lick their wounds. In the fall of 1814 a war that had begun with much huffing and puffing finally ended in a stalemate. Not even the hawks in Congress thought the cost worth the effort any longer. In effect, both sides declared victory and moved on to more pressing business. And in some senses both sides did win. The American diplomats who outsmarted the British at the peace conference gained huge territorial concessions, while the Canadian militiamen's spirited defense against an armed invasion contributed significantly to the formation of a distinct Canadian consciousness. *City of Toronto Art Collection*

The Rebellion of 1837

In December of 1837 an army of self-styled Upper Canada "republicans" rose up against the Family Compact, the system of oligarchic cronyism imposed by Her Majesty's Government. (Rebels appeared in Lower Canada as well, but in that province French-Canadian nationalism was the main impetus.) William Lyon Mackenzie, a journalist who had been inspired by the best ideals of American democracy, was the driving force behind the rebellion in Upper Canada. After uprisings in Toronto and Kingston were suppressed, Mackenzie fled to the U.S., where he continued the fight. *AO*

Josiah Henson and Mrs. Henson, 1877. One of the reasons the rebellion failed was that too many Canadians remembered their earlier treatment under American rule. Among the earliest anti-rebel volunteers was former slave Josiah Henson, whose autobiography had helped inspire Harriet Beecher Stowe to write *Uncle Tom's Cabin*. Henson organized a black militia troop, which rushed to the defense of Fort Malden in Amherstburg. Native nations also were quick to volunteer. *MTRL*

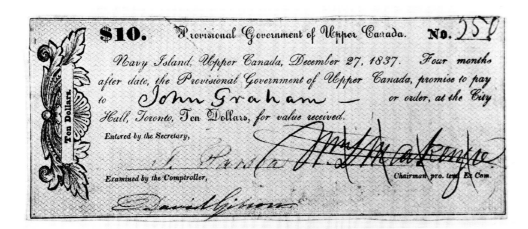

As part of the plan to take over power, Mackenzie's "provincial government" issued its own scrip, although by December 27, when this ten-dollar certificate was signed and dated, the rebels were already in exile on Navy Island in the Niagara River. Needless to say, the bill was never cashed. *AO*

"December 29, 1837: Bloodthirsty Canadians send the Steamer Caroline over Niagara Falls. Scores of innocent men, women and children plunge to a horrible death."

Or so American newspapers depicted the destruction of a steamer on which the rebels were ferrying supplies to Navy Island. In truth, the crew had fled after the boat was seized by Canadian raiders, no passengers were aboard, and the vessel broke up before reaching the falls. But an American ship had been attacked in American waters and the international incident that blew up led to red faces in Whitehall and suspension of the officer responsible for the raid. *MTRL*

The Fenian Invasions

In 1866, an Irish-American organization, the Fenian Brotherhood, turned its eyes toward Canada—for one more year, a colony of their hereditary enemy, Britain.

> *We are a Fenian brotherhood,*
> *skilled in the arts of war,*
> *And we're going to fight for Ireland,*
> *the land that we adore.*
> *Many battles have we won,*
> *along with the boys in blue,*
> *And we'll go and capture Canada,*
> *for we've nothing else to do.*
>
> Fenian marching song

They may have liked to sing, but these were far from comic opera Irishmen. Irish immigrants who had served in the ranks of both the Union and Confederate Armies in the recent American Civil War provided a large pool of battle-toughened veterans. By contrast, Canadian militias consisted of mainly untrained volunteers, many still in their teens. But when nearly a thousand well-armed Fenians launched a raid from Buffalo on the night of May 31, 1866, landing just above Fort Erie, these young Canadian amateurs were sure their moment for glory had come. They rushed to their country's defense and were promptly driven off the field in a disorderly heap.

The Fenian success at the Battle of Ridgeway proved ephemeral. Without supply lines, and in the face of large-scale Canadian mobilization, the Irishmen were soon forced to retreat back across the border. Four years later, when the group made another attempt, the Canadian military was ready, and the brief glory days of the Fenian brotherhood were over. Except, of course, in song and story.

The Battle of Pelee Island, painted by C. H. Forster. On February 26, 1838, a group of self-designated "freedom fighters" from Sandusky, Ohio, crossed the frozen lake in an attempt to capture Pelee Island. Canadian militia from Leamington promptly set off to confront them, marching through the icy darkness by lantern light. Thirty-one men lost their lives in the ensuing struggle, which ended with the rebels fleeing back to Ohio. In the long run, however, Mackenzie's efforts helped push the British into liberalizing the governance of Canada. Mackenzie spent ten years in exile in the States, then was pardoned and returned to Ontario. Now a hero, he was elected to the provincial parliament as member for the Lake Erie riding of Haldimand. *PC/FMHS*

Many University of Toronto colleges had their own militia companies. One of these was the Queen's Own Rifles, who hurried down to the station to take the train to war, toasting their good fortune all the way. Some of the boys look as if they had barely started to shave. *AO*

After the battle, one boastful Fenian snatched up an abandoned enemy rifle and dashed it to the ground, declaring that this was the way he'd treat all Canadians. The gun went off and killed him. Alexander Von Erichsen, an artist traveling with the Fenians, was standing by to record the incident. *FEMB*

53

Erie, Pennsylvania, also owed its growth to a new waterway—the Erie Extension Canal, which connected the Ohio River city of Pittsburgh to the lake. This photo, taken by Walter Scott, dates from 1852, making it one of the earliest exterior shots.
C. B. Hall Collection, ECHS

Chapter Three

BOOM TIMES BEGIN—
THE AMERICAN SHORE, 1815-1880

The War of 1812 was over. Momentous border issues had been settled, the reputations of two future presidents (William Henry Harrison and Andrew Jackson) established, folk heroes (Laura Secord, Perry, Brock, Tecumseh) created. Erie was open for business, but where were the customers? Beyond a few scattered settlements on both sides of the lake lay only deep woods and more deep woods. A generous estimate of the south shore's population, with Detroit thrown in for good measure, might be some five thousand isolated souls. And yet little more than a decade later, Erie's lonely woodlands and swamps were being transformed into the greatest boom town the world had ever seen. Pioneers from the east were now opting for the Great Lakes region, even as new waves of immigrants were setting out across the ocean to follow in their footsteps. A popular song told the story:

Oh, the Er-i-e was a-risin'
The gin was agettin' low.
And I scarcely think we'll get a little drink
Til we get to Buffalo-oh-oh, till we get to Buffalo.

A canal across New York State to connect the Hudson River with Lake Erie and open up the Great Lakes region was not a new idea, but until DeWitt Clinton became governor in 1817 no one in high office had taken it seriously. (Jefferson declared that to "talk of making a canal three hundred and fifty miles through a wilderness is little short of madness," and his successor, James Madison, vetoed a bill to assist the state in building it.) But the governor forced the plan through, and the nascent American entrepreneurial spirit quickly took hold, as people caught on that "Clinton's Ditch" was a bonanza in the making. Thousands of newly arrived immigrants, mainly Irish and German, rushed to apply for construction jobs on the canal. Lumbermen, sawmill workers, stone quarrymen and masons suddenly found their services in constant demand.

It was clear that the community selected as the canal's western terminus would also become the region's leading metropolis, and as work progressed a battle to the death shaped up between the various lake villages. Every type of political pressure was ruthlessly employed, from bribery to threats of

DeWitt Clinton, father of the Erie Canal.
A Pictorial History of the Great Lakes

George Catlin's print showing the primitive and highly dangerous methods of canal construction at Lockport, just east of Buffalo. *New York Historical Society*

Down the lake, villages like Dunkirk, Erie, Ashtabula, Painesville, Lorain, Huron, and Sandusky were turning into small cities almost overnight. They all were heavily dependent on water transport; once you left the plush steamers and packet boats and tried to make your way overland, travel became more problematical—and uncomfortable. In an account of his 1842 tour, Charles Dickens gives a bone-crunching description of what it was like traveling the western roads in a stagecoach.

At one time we were all flung together in a heap at the bottom of the coach, and at another we were crushing our heads against the roof. Now one side was deep in the mire, and we were holding on to the other . . . A great portion . . . is over a corduroy road, which is made by throwing trunks of trees into a marsh, and leaving them to settle there. The very slightest of the jolts with which the carriage fell from log to log was enough to have dislocated all the bones in the human body. . .

For now, the building of roads took a back seat. Having seen what canals could do for a region, the citizens of western Ohio and Indiana concluded that they needed some of their own. Why shouldn't they share in the economic boom? Before long, canals were being dug in a dozen different directions, among them the Miami, connecting the lake port of Toledo and the river port of Cincinnati, and the Wabash and Erie, which ran west to the Wabash River from the Maumee at a point just south of Toledo.

Small fortunes were being made by bankers and engineers, merchants and hoteliers, but it was the exporters of raw materials like timber who were really profiting. By mid-century, unimaginable numbers of logs were washing down Canadian and American streams toward the lake. Some of the lumber was used in Erie lake ports, some went west to Chicago, and the rest was floated east on barges or in great log armadas to Tonawanda, where it was milled and shipped to the Atlantic Coast via the Erie Canal. Tonawanda, adjacent to Buffalo, became a great lumber center through a fluke

bodily harm. In the end, Buffalo won out over its fiercest competitor, the adjacent hamlet of Black Rock. (The victor became the "Queen City," while the vanquished eventually lost its separate identity.)

Buffalo felt the canal boom at once. Travelers needed not just restaurants and hotels but banks, pawn shops, trading posts, dry goods stores, and wharves where lake vessels could dock. And the tradesmen, in turn, required houses and hospitals and schools. In 1835, a leading builder, Benjamin Rathbun (also, as it turned out, one of the city's leading embezzlers), reported that his company had erected ninety-nine new buildings. Among them were fifty-two stores, thirty-two residences, a theater and a large hotel. During the 1830s and 1840s, an estimated one thousand people a day were arriving via the canal; some stayed, most continued on west, but all contributed to Buffalo's growth.

The lock at Lockport as a barge arrives. Lockport demonstrated the economic benefits of a canal. Before the workmen arrived, there were two houses here; ten years after the canal opened, the population had soared to six thousand. *George Virtue, London*

of geography. Located just up the Niagara River, it was protected from the worst effects of the notorious storm surges that periodically crashed into Buffalo's harbor and which were capable of throwing an entire harborful of lumber a dozen blocks into the city. In 1890, Tonawanda temporarily dethroned Chicago as the world's number-one lumber port.

> *Come all you bold sailors that follow the lakes*
> *On an iron ore vessel your living to make*
> *I shipped in Chicago, bid adieu to the shore*
> *Bound away to Escanaba for red iron ore.*

> *. . . Now the Roberts's in Cleveland, made fast stem and stern*
> *And over the bottle we'll spin a big yarn,*
> *But Captain Harvey Shannon had ought to stand treat*
> *For getting to Cleveland ahead of the fleet.*
> *Derry down, down, down, derry down.*

Along with the bold sailors, up-and-coming industrialists also headed for Cleveland after the Civil War. Shipping magnate Alva Bradley relocated from Vermilion to build the largest fleet on the lakes. Jephtha Wade moved down from Michigan and founded the Western Union Telegraph Company. Charles Brush, born in a crossroads just outside Cleveland, invented the arc lamp and later joined forces with Thomas Edison to create General Electric.

Other lake cities weren't far behind. Toledo's Edward Drummond Libbey established the glass industry. In Buffalo, Henry Wells and William Fargo organized a pair of delivery services, one called Wells, Fargo and the other American Express. B. F. Goodrich built the first rubber tire factory in an Ohio Canal town 30 miles south of Cleveland, and with Harvey Firestone turned Akron into the world's rubber capital. For good measure, add Detroit's Henry Ford and Pittsburgh's Carnegie, Frick, Westinghouse, and Mellon. The world watched in wonder as these self-made and supremely confident dynamos inspired each other to ever greater entrepreneurial heights.

Lola Montez : Culture came calling as well as commerce. Charles Dickens and William Makepeace Thackeray arrived on tour to read from their latest works; Ralph Waldo Emerson, Louis Agassiz and Oliver Wendell Holmes lectured; the legendary *demimondaine* Lola Montez brought her colorful theatrical troupe, as did the great English actors William Macready and Junius Booth and their celebrated American competitor, Edwin Forrest. *Munchen Stadtmuseum*

Many other man-made waterways would follow, but it was the Erie Canal that caught the popular imagination. Ballads sprang to the lips of itinerant singers, newspapers printed celebratory editorials, and amateur painters depicted scenes like this anonymous view of the canal at Tonawanda. When it finally opened on a brisk October day in 1825, entire villages turned out to celebrate the arrival of the first packet boat. As one old-timer recalled the day, "A salute was fired from a cannon as the *Seneca Chief*, drawn by nine handsome gray horses, passed through here on her initial trip, having on board no less distinguished a personage than the governor, who conveyed a keg of water from Lake Erie to mingle with those of the Hudson River. It was a grand event, and one never to be forgotten." *HST*

Cleveland Town Hall, 1839. When guest speaker DeWitt Clinton turned the first spade for the Ohio Canal in 1825, he predicted great days ahead, stating that Cleveland would gain access "not only to the markets of New Orleans, but of Philadelphia, Baltimore, and Montreal". He wasn't exaggerating; Cleveland would almost immediately catch up and surpass its rival at the eastern end of the lake. By the time the new canal opened in 1833, the population of this muddy port at the mouth of the perpetually silted-up Cuyahoga River was already approaching five thousand. Just twenty years later it had risen an incredible eight hundred percent to more than forty thousand, and the new metropolis could boast of a splendid, newly dredged harbor and a fine town hall. Perhaps the most striking statistic of all is that according to the 1840 census, Ohio had become the third most populous state in the union. *CPL*

Many of the Irish and German canal workers, their work on the big ditch finished, decided that they liked the area and turned their considerable skills to helping build the growing city of Buffalo. Their children found jobs in the burgeoning lumber industry. The log rafters in this 1867 photo of Tonawanda Harbor are, from left to right: Matt Scanlon, Pat Scanlon, Daniel Burd, William Sutton and Martin Scanlon, in the company of an unidentified colleague. Chances are he, too, had an Irish name. *HST*

DAILY LINE OF OHIO CANAL PACKETS

Between Cleveland & Portsmouth.

DISTANCE 309 MILES—THROUGH IN 80 HOURS.

A Packet of this Line leaves Cleveland every day at 4 o'clock P. M. and Portsmouth every day at 9 o'clock A. M.

T. INGRAHAM, *Office foot of Superior-street, Cleveland,*
OTIS & CURTIS, *General Stage Office,* do. } AGENTS.
G. J. LEET, ... *Portsmouth,*

NEIL, MOORE & CO.'S Line of Stages leaves Cleveland daily for Columbus, via Wooster and Hebron.
OTIS & CURTIS' Line of Stages leaves Cleveland daily for Pittsburgh, Buffalo, Detroit and Wellsville.

When a north-south canal to connect the lake with the Ohio River was first proposed, another municipal bloodletting occurred, this time among the villages of Sandusky, Cleveland, Lorain, Ohio City, Vermilion and Painesville. Cleveland's selection as the new canal's northern outlet assured that settlement's dominance of the central basin. It's strange to think that if the decision had gone another way, today's big-league sports teams might be known as the Vermilion Indians or the Painesville Browns. And the Rock 'n' Roll Hall of Fame, which enshrines Elvis and Buddy and Bo, might be located in Sandusky or Lorain. *Cleveland Public Library*

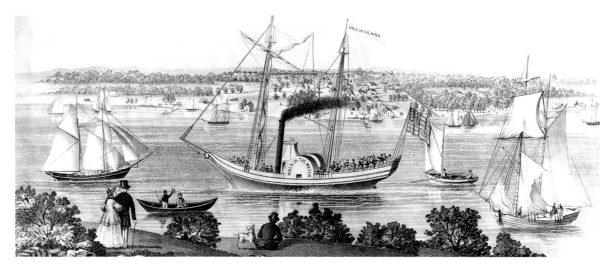

Detroit was also rapidly expanding. These two views, made sixteen years apart, show how fast the scene was changing. In the earlier one, the *Walk-in-the-Water*— built in Black Rock in 1818 and the first steam vessel to sail the lake—is shown making her regular Buffalo–Michigan run in 1820. (She would founder and be lost off Point Abino, just west of Buffalo, the following year.) Detroit is visible in the background, still little more than a village. The second view, an 1836 painting by William Bennett, depicts a harbor crowded with vessels, and beyond them a solid mass of buildings. By the 1850s, the population of the once-desolate frontier post was nearing fifty thousand. *MTRL, Lore of the Lakes*

We get a hint of the era's dynamism by following the career of a typical immigrant of the times. His name was John Lathers (pictured here as an elderly man), and in 1830 he left Coote Hill, County Cavan, Ireland, to try his luck in the New World. After four years in Paterson, New Jersey, working as a master machinist, the young Irishman had saved enough money to buy 160 acres of farmland, at $1.25 an acre, in the wilds of Michigan. When a few years later his six younger brothers and sisters decided to join him, Lathers sent a detailed letter explaining just how they were to go about tracking down his faraway homestead. The letter evokes a sense of the new man John Lathers has now become. Born into the timeless realities of the still half-medieval Irish countryside, where the lord of the manor regulated every aspect of life and livelihood, he has evolved into an American, tilling his own land and creating his own destiny. He takes the madcap speed at which the world is evolving—steamboats, railroads, canals, and all the rest—for granted, and is more than a little patronizing to his less-worldly siblings back home. *Dearborn Historical Museum*

If you are all coming out . . . fetch your beds and also some cooking utensils. Also fetch as much coarse cloth wearing clothes as will be sufficient for two or three years . . . And when you leave home do not let your mind be known to everyone you meet with. Whatever money you have you should either have it sewed in a belt or some part of your clothes ...When you come to New York, do not throw away your cooking utensils, for you can use them on the way. When in New York take your passage to Albany on the steamboat [on the Hudson River] . . . When you get to Albany take passage on the Western (Erie) Canal and be careful they do not charge you an over price. The regular price is one cent and a half per mile; the distance is 363 miles. When you get to Buffalo take your passage on the steamboat for Detroit. When you come to Detroit get your baggage on the railroad cars for Dearborn ... When you leave Dearborn go 4 miles west on the Chicago Turnpike, where you will find a large house painted red known by the name of Ruff's Tavern. Pass that a very short distance and you will find a road turning to the right hand, 2 miles and you will be where we live...

Lathers lived on into his nineties, long enough to become friendly with a neighbor born and raised on another farm just down the road, a likely looking young man by the name of Henry Ford. *Authors' collection*

An ad for Toledo's Bailey Brothers Shipyard, c. 1870 *HCGL*

A Sandusky shipyard in 1880. *LOL*

Unfortunately for those poised to strike it rich on yet more canals, no sooner had bargemen begun reworking the old ditties ("Got'n old mule, her name is Sal/Fifteen miles on the Wabash Canal") then a new tune could be heard across the fields and valleys, growing louder with every beat of the hammer ("In eighteen hundred and forty-one/work on the railroad just begun/I put my corduroy britches on/to work upon the railroad"). The iron horse had arrived. In this 1850 lithograph of Ashtabula Harbor, a toy-like train is emerging from behind a warehouse on the right. But it was clear that the railroads were far from child's play: they were the future. *CPL*

Citizens of the lake ports were briefly plunged into despair over the coming of rail travel, but optimism revived when it became apparent that trains could not yet compete with cheaper water transport. The 1856 survey of working vessels on Lake Erie in Lloyd's Steamboat Directory lists no less than 238 steamers and propellers (steam ships substituting an Ericsson screw for the paddle wheel) along with 1,149 cargo-carrying sailing vessels, a figure that included 608 schooners, 211 brigs, and 290 sloops and scows—almost all of them launched from Lake Erie shipyards. Cleveland Harbor, seen in this 1874 picture, was filled to capacity. No wonder boat builders and shippers were whistling as they worked. *HCGL*

Shipyards experimented with ingenious conversions of older vessels to accommodate modern needs. The oddly rigged *Harlem*, built in the 1830s, had three masts as well as two small smokestacks tucked away together at the stern. *LOL*

The *Africa* (1873) was something of a late hybrid, a propeller vessel that was also a three-master. It broke up and went down with thirteen hands during a heavy gale in 1895. *UWO*

The *Unadilla* began life in 1862 as a schooner, but was converted into a schooner barge by the removal of its masts. Here, loaded with cedar posts, the vessel is ready to be towed east on the Erie Canal. *HST*

Dock wallopers in charge of handling the endless piles of milled lumber pose for their photo at Tonawanda in 1899. The stiff leather aprons are for protection of their private parts, and a good thing, too, judging from the angle at which they received the railroad ties for stacking. Shingles and lathing were also produced in vast quantities. J. S. Bliss & Company, the second-largest manufacturer of shingles in the world, turned out fifty-six million in a single season. *HST*

Captain Peter Johnson and wife Mary, with their daughter Agnes (between them), sit down for dinner aboard the lumber barge *Isabel Reed*, 1897. *HST*

The *Viking*, a lumber hooker out of Tonawanda, towed barges loaded with timber. *HST*

With more land being cleared for farming, ungainly yet somehow appealing grain elevators began to rise along the major waterfronts. Cleveland became the outlet for Ohio's fertile farmland, as did Detroit for Michigan. But since all the eastbound grain transporters had to offload at Buffalo, that city profited to an even greater extent and became the hub of grain transport. In the morning mist, a tugboat steams through Buffalo's Elevator Alley in 1927. *AO*

Beyond timber and grain, a new industry was waiting to emerge. The discovery of enormous iron-ore deposits along Lake Superior had caused great excitement; all the fuel anyone could want for the production of iron and steel could be found in the coal mines of the nearby Appalachian foothills. All that was lacking was an efficient way to process the ore, and the patenting of the Bessemer system in England in 1856 solved that problem. Almost immediately, gigantic coke-fired blast furnaces in the major cities began spewing out tons of metal. This is an early Otis Steel plant in Cleveland, c. 1885, seen from the Clark Avenue Bridge. *CPL*

A new type of lake vessel made its debut in 1879. The Cleveland-built *RJ Hackett* became the first dedicated long-length Great Lakes ore carrier. The wooden propeller vessel measured 208 feet and weighed 748 tons, and was soon followed by a fleet of sister ships. *HCGL*

John D. Rockefeller *Rockefeller Family Archives*

A new word, tycoon—from the Chinese meaning "military commander"—entered the language around this time, and journalists were quick to apply it to the hard-nosed heroes of industry coming to prominence. The relentless John D. Rockefeller became the prototype. His family came to Cleveland from upstate New York when he was beginning high school, where his best (and, by most accounts, only) friend was the future robber baron Marcus Hanna. Starting as a commodities broker, Rockefeller saw more potential in oil, and before reaching his thirtieth birthday had created a company uniting all the various strands of oil manufacture—exploration, recovery, refining and distribution—under a single corporate umbrella. In the process, he crushed any competitor that refused his offer to be bought out. He called his new company Standard Oil, and in 1870 built his first refinery, seen above that same year, along the Cuyahoga River. The oil came from Rockefeller's newly discovered wells in western Pennsylvania. *CPL*

Rockefeller had demonstrated that empire building could be a young man's game. A pair of Cleveland kids in their twenties, Henry Sherwin (left) and E. P. Williams, emphasized the point when they got together, also in 1870, to reinvent the American paint industry. By the turn of the century, Sherwin-Williams had become the largest paint and varnish producer in the world. In these portraits we see the youthful Sherwin the year the company was founded, and Williams in 1872. The partners' innovations, especially their development of the first durable outdoor paint, revolutionized the industry. They followed Rockefeller's example in consolidating production and distribution; in the tin can plant, shown here c. 1890, they manufactured their own containers instead of relying on an outside source. *Sherwin-Williams Company Archives*

Emigration to
CANADA.

MEMORANDUM of the terms on which the Government has agreed to convey a limited number of Settlers from Ireland to Upper-Canada, under the superintendance of *Mr. Robinson* and to locate them upon lands in that Province ; and also of the conditions upon which lands shall be granted.

Such Emigrants as the *Superintendant* shall accept, shall be conveyed from the place of embarkation in Ireland, to their lands in *Upper-Canada*, wholly at the public charge, and provisions shall be furnished them during their voyage, and for one whole year after their location upon their respective lots.

Chapter Four

THE CANADIAN SIDE, 1820-1945

Part One—The Sweep of History

Anna Jameson, an intrepid British writer who toured the area in 1837, was left starry-eyed by the enterprising Yanks she encountered in Buffalo and Detroit. The inhabitants of the Canadian shoreline, however, did not create as favorable an impression. Up there, Mrs. Jameson found, "A lethargic spell seems to have bound up the energies of the people . . . all the symptoms of apathy, indolence, mistrust, hopelessness!" She was driven to ask, "Can I, or any one, help wondering at the difference and asking whence it arrives?"

Her description seems a bit harsh. If Canadian society was less aggressively entrepreneurial than its American counterpart, it still had its own sort of applied energy; the challenges of survival in the deep woods made it unlikely that anyone could be apathetic or indolent for long. A memorial cairn in the Port Ryerse churchyard sums it up, paying a deserved tribute to the people who "braved the loneliness of the unknown wilderness . . . cleared the forest, blazed the roads, bridged the fords, drained the swamps . . . sacrificed and endured that their inheritors might enjoy in peace and comfort the fruits of their toil." Despite her prejudices,

An 1825 immigration advertisement posted in Cork, Ireland.
Peterborough Centennial Museum and Archives

The task of clearing a space large enough for a small house and a few crops must have appeared overwhelming at first. There were endless trees to fell, scavenging wild animals, huge flocks of birds attacking the crops, and sudden blizzards sweeping down from the far north. This 1837 Essex County watercolor by Philip John Bainbrigge gives a sense of what the first settlers were up against. *NAC*

Mrs. Jameson was onto a significant element in the Canadian-American nexus. Americans may have been too busy nation-building to notice, but even at this early date Canadians were already finding it necessary to perform a psychological balancing

One side of the lake had nature in abundance; the other side had tens of thousands of inhabitants, many with money in their pockets, looking for a temporary escape from crowded city streets. As early as the 1820s, excursion boats were setting out from Buffalo to nearby Canadian beaches, and by 1833 there were regular runs to the idyllic precincts of Port Stanley, halfway down the lake. The plush Fraser House Hotel on the fashionable heights at Port Stanley, c. 1880, was a favorite of visitors from Cleveland. *UWO*

act between their country and their neighbor to the south. The seductive call of American economic freedom and one-man, one-vote democracy wafted across the lake. Set against that was the appeal of British law and custom, with its emphasis on fairness and civic responsibility. Both systems had their drawbacks—the worst excesses of dog-eat-dog capitalism in the former, a tenacious class system in the other. Most of the early settlers predictably clung to the Crown and all it represented, but future generations would often turn their eyes southward in search of greater opportunity.

The society that grew up along the northern shore in those early days was isolated and conservative. It was also, not surprisingly, full of peculiar characters. Take, for example, Dr. John Troyer, the leading citizen of Port Rowan, on Long Point Bay, around the turn of the nineteenth century. Troyer was a respected botanist, healer and agricultural pioneer; he was also known to sleep with a bear trap bolted to the floor alongside his bed. He needed it, he shamefacedly explained to his friends, to discourage attacks from the local witches, who liked nothing better than to transform him into a horse and ride him across the lake's frozen surface to wild Yankee revels in Dunkirk, New York. Although Troyer was by no means the leading eccentric along this stretch of lakeshore. Pride of place on that particular list would soon go to Colonel Thomas Talbot.

Boats docked in Port Colborne Harbor, waiting to pass through the Welland Canal, 1870. In 1824, an influential St. Catharine's businessman named William Merritt founded the Welland Canal Company. The new canal would connect Lake Ontario and Lake Erie, bypassing Niagara Falls and providing access to the continental interior for Lower Canada and the American northeast. When the Welland opened in 1829, it proved an enormous success, and a mere dozen years later the government enlarged it to allow steamers through. Of the many canals dug along the lake in the early nineteenth century, only the Welland, a key link in the St. Lawrence Seaway system, remains in use today. *PCHMM*

Main street in winter, Dunnville, c. 1900. One of the towns that came into existence because of the Welland Canal was Dunnville. The picturesque river port was founded in 1828 by Salmon Minor, an American who happened to be taking a short cut to Michigan when he learned that a feeder canal linking the Grand River to the Welland would begin right where he was standing. He saw his opportunity and went no farther. *DDHA*

An 1859 advertising poster from Ogdensburg, N.Y., on the St. Lawrence River, demonstrates the central role the Welland Canal played in Great Lakes shipping. Without it, this company, and a multitude of others, would not have existed. *PDHM*

Lighthouse keeping was by definition a lonely job, and David Fortier, who took over the Port Colborne lighthouse from his father in 1865 and held it until his death in 1911, looks like a man more comfortable with the winds and waves than with human society. Although his wife, Jennie, seems sociable enough in this 1870 family portrait. *PCHMM*

By the 1850s, large volumes of Canadian wheat and other grains were being sent east. In 1859, the Grand Trunk Railway built a grain elevator at Port Colborne, where schooners like the *MF Merrick*, seen here in 1864, brought their loads for transfer to rail cars. *PCHMM*

SHIPPED, in apparent good order and condition, by *E. & Ryerse*   for account and risk of whom it may concern, on board of the *Schr. Rebecca Foster* whereof *Abraham Fish* is Master, now lying at this Port, and bound for *Buffalo*   the following and annexed articles, marked and numbered as per margin, all of which are to be delivered as addressed, in like order and condition, at the aforesaid Port, unto the Consignees, or to   Assigns, (the dangers of Navigation, Fire, and acts of Providence excepted): the freight and charges to be paid as mentioned below. In witness whereof the Master of said vessel hath *subscribed two* Bill of Lading of this tenor and date.

MARKS AND NUMBERS.	QUANTITY AND DESCRIPTION OF GOODS.	OWNERS.	CONSIGNEES.
1817	15/60 Bus.ʰ Wheat	Simpson McCall Victoria	H. Sherwood & Buffalo
	Freight five cents pr Bushel payable in New York funds		
		A. Leask	

A bill of lading for another 1864 grain carrier, the *Rebecca Foster*, out of Port Ryerse. The schooner was headed for the grain elevators at Buffalo with 1,817 bushels of wheat. The bill lists as owner a Mr. Ryerse, no doubt a son or grandson of the original United Empire Loyalist couple who settled in the area. *AC*

Industry was not completely absent from the Canadian shoreline. One busy smelter was the Normandale Foundry, which ran from 1818 to 1847, when the ore from a nearby bog finally ran out. The operation turned out large numbers of plows and other iron implements, as well as an iron stove in great demand across Ontario and in the American Midwest. *NHS/EBDM*

Newspaper advertisement in Toronto Patriot, March 1838, indicates quantity of production

A bombastic Anglo-Irish aristocrat, Thomas Talbot resigned his army commission in 1800 in order to return to Ontario, where he had served a few years earlier. Despite his small stature, he had a high opinion of his appearance and talents. ("None are more manly than I," he once informed his bemused commanding officer.) Back in Canada, Talbot used family connections to sell the Upper Canada government on a scheme whereby for every 100 acres of his own land that he sublet to a new settler he would receive an additional 200 for himself. He amassed a personal demesne of more than 60,000 acres of prime farmland along the central basin. His stewardship extended from Port Rowan to Port Talbot and inland as far as St. Thomas (the latter two among the many places he had named after himself). Here he ruled as an absolute, if erratic, potentate, doling out strips of land to people of his choosing, a group that emphatically did not include Americans, liberals, or anyone insufficiently respectful. Portrait by James D. Wandesford. *McIntosh Gallery/UWO*

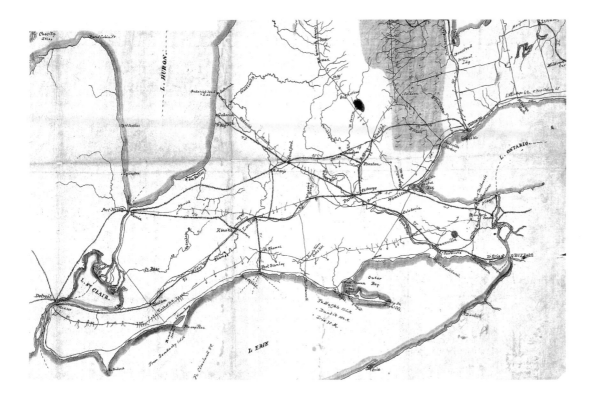

The leisurely pace of development in southwestern Ontario is made visible in this 1866 road and railway map. Talbot Street runs just north of the lake from Port Rowan to Rondeau. The Great Western Railway runs roughly parallel to it farther inland. Talbot Street remains the primary lakeshore route. *NAC*

After Talbot retreated to a sulky retirement in the 1840s, much of his domain was taken over by a collection of rowdy characters who might not have been tolerated when the fusty tyrant ruled the roost. This 1858 picture of Port Burwell, for which the entire population seems to have turned out, has a touch of the American Wild West about it. The men in front of the Frontier House and Tavern might be mistaken for a Dodge City marshal and his deputies. *PBMM*

Just down the road from Port Burwell was Long Point. By mid-century the sandy peninsula had degenerated into a northern version of the Barbary Coast. It was infamous as a place where pirate gangs altered signal lights to drive vessels onto sand bars, gambling dens and bordellos were plentiful, brawls were commonplace, unwary sailors were often robbed and occasionally murdered, and criminals on the run found a safe haven. The sporting element from Buffalo, Cleveland and Detroit were also regular visitors, crossing the lake in their yachts to take in events like this 1858 bare-knuckle prizefight between two men named Morrissey and the Benicia Boy. Boxing was illegal in both Canada and the U.S. at the time, but that didn't stop the New York-based Frank Leslie's *Illustrated Newspaper* from sending an artist to record the epic battle. *NAC*

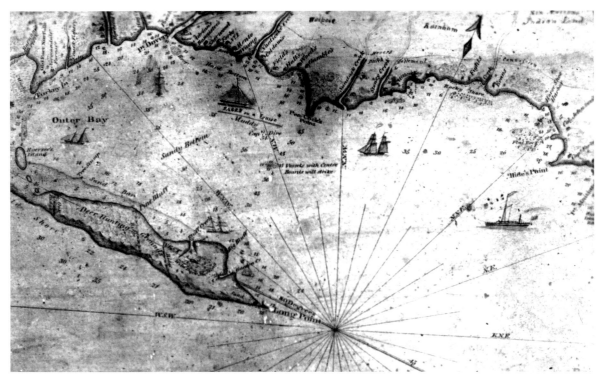

"All the Lake Ontario captains on both sides and the Erie captains on the American side are afraid of the north shore," commented Captain Alexander McNeilledge in the preface to his 1848 *Chart and Sailing Instructions for the North Shore of Lake Erie*. His journal filled a need, for without the captain's well-observed navigational instructions and maps, like this one of Long Point Bay, many more vessels would have joined the underwater fleet. *Courtesy of Peter Knechtel*

Not everyone at Long Point was a hardened criminal. Abigail and Jeremiah Becker were among the few settlers trying to scratch out a living from the land. One stormy night in December of 1854, the twenty-three-year-old Abigail was alone with her young children when she heard cries from a ship aground on the outer bar. Rushing outside, she made out eight men clinging to a schooner's icy rigging. She built a bonfire to guide her, and though she could not swim and was weighed down by voluminous petticoats, lunged repeatedly through the 10-foot swells to drag the exhausted seamen to safety. Sailors around the lake contributed to a five-hundred-dollar purse, which was presented to her at a dinner in Buffalo. Queen Victoria chipped in with 50 pounds and a medal for the "Angel of Long Point." She used the money to buy a farm on the mainland. Her feckless husband, now turned poacher, stayed where he was and a few winters later froze to death. Abigail lived until 1905, having raised nineteen children, although she received no medals for that act of personal heroism. *NHS/EBD*

Not far off the tip of the point, Erie takes a deep plunge to 214 feet. The most storied of the lake's many ship disasters took place here one foggy night in August, 1852, when the elegant steamer *Atlantic*, carrying hundreds of Wisconsin-bound Norwegian immigrants, collided with a cargo ship. Evacuation was proceeding calmly when the Scandinavians, unable to understand the crew's instructions, began throwing themselves over the side. In a short time panic overcame the rest of the passengers, despite every attempt by the crew to restrain them. Over three hundred lives were lost, and hundreds of thousands of dollars in cash and precious metals were rumored to have gone down with the ship. The wreck of the *Atlantic* was discovered in the mid-1980s by Port Dover divers, although whether the riches were found remains a mystery. *PC/FMHS*

In 1866 a group of wealthy hunters decided to do something about Long Point. They bought up most of the 20-mile sand spit, used their political influence to run the criminals off, and closed the Point to everyone else. They even restricted themselves to two weeks of duck hunting per year. Because of these simultaneously enlightened and self-serving policies, most of Long Point has remained frozen in time for nearly a century and a half. Here we see Edward Harris (right) and a friend, two of the Long Point millionaires, after a day's shooting in 1877. *AC*

Ferry service between Black Rock (Buffalo) and Bridgeburg (Fort Erie) was established shortly after the end of the War of 1812. As settlement increased, similar services sprang up everywhere. The ferry fleet ranged from small steam vessels like the *Louise*, which cruised around Point Pelee and the western islands, to the busy Detroit–Windsor commuter ferry, and finally the massive "city-of" steamers (*City of Cleveland*, *City of Erie*, *City of Detroit*, *City of Buffalo*, and City of nearly everything else). This last group were technically not ferries, but made regular runs between the larger cities. *PC/PPNP, NAC*

There were also numerous small boats for hire, such as the one being used for this Long Point fishing expedition, August 1923. *AO*

Cargo ships often carried passengers. The *Shenango #1* was a rail-car ferry whose daily run took her from Erie to Port Dover and back. These two late-1890s photos show a view from the bridge of the *Shenango #1* and a group of Port Doverites enjoying dinner as they return from the American side. A few years later, in January of 1905, the ship became icebound off Conneaut, Ohio, and burned to the water line when the crew tried to keep warm by feeding the furnace. *NHS/EBDM*

Every port of any size had a rail line that ran right up to its docks. Here trains and boats meet at the Port Dover harbor, c. 1895. *Courtesy of Peter Knechtel*

The steamer *Ashtabula* entering Port Burwell harbor, c. 1910. The steamer carried rail cars from its namesake city in Ohio across to Port Burwell, Ontario, where the coal-filled cars were coupled to trains headed for Canadian cities. This daily crossing continued for more than fifty years. *PBMM*

During much of the late nineteenth century and early twentieth, tourism and industry shared a history at Erieau. Regular excursion boats brought visitors from Cleveland to enjoy the lush beauty of the Rondeau peninsula, while not far away the Pere Marquette Railroad Company used the port as a major coal distribution site. *NAC*

When the International Bridge, built by Sir Casimir Gzowski, was opened in 1873 over the Niagara River, it was hailed as one of the engineering wonders of the world. One feature was the Dummy, a motorless self-propelled single-car commuter trolley that ran on rechargeable batteries. For sixty years it crossed and re-crossed the river from Black Rock to Bridgeburg and back, at its mid-twenties height making twenty-two round trips a day, first run at 6:10 A.M., last at 11:55 P.M. In this 1875 photo, conductor Enoch Bone stands proudly at the front of his charge. Seven years later another conductor failed to notice that the rarely used swing section of the bridge had been opened, and the Dummy fell through onto a bridge abutment, crushing two passengers. *FEMB*

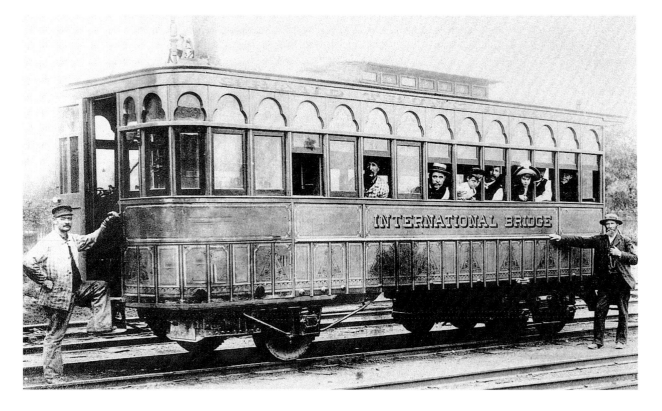

The popular Leamington–Kingsville streetcar line, connecting two ports some six miles apart at the western end of the lake, was typical of the interurbans that came into use with the arrival of electric power. The original owner of this picture accidentally tore it, but was so fond of the view that he carefully pasted it back together. By the early twentieth century, dozens of lines on both sides of the lake created a spider web of tracks that could take you in any direction. *PC/FMHS*

Interior of an L & PS car in its plush heyday, c. 1920. Stained-glass window arches and classic joinery added a note of elegance.
Prothero

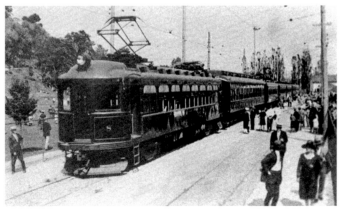

The L & PS Line (the London and Port Stanley, or on a bad day, the Late and Poor Service Line). In this 1920s photo, passengers from London have just debarked at the last stop, a dance pavilion that by no small coincidence happened to be owned by the railway. Until the 1950s, teenagers in the small lake port took the train into London to attend high school. *Courtesy of Frank and Nancy Prothero*

American interurbans were less stately, but usually more up to date. This club car on a Cleveland interurban, c. 1930, offers both cards and sightseeing. *NAC*

When Canadians put on their glad rags to go downtown, the downtowns they visited were likely to be in Buffalo or Cleveland or Erie. Here, a day ferry returns to Port Dover, c. 1910. It is probably a Sunday, judging from the number of people assembled to watch the boat arrive. *PDHM*

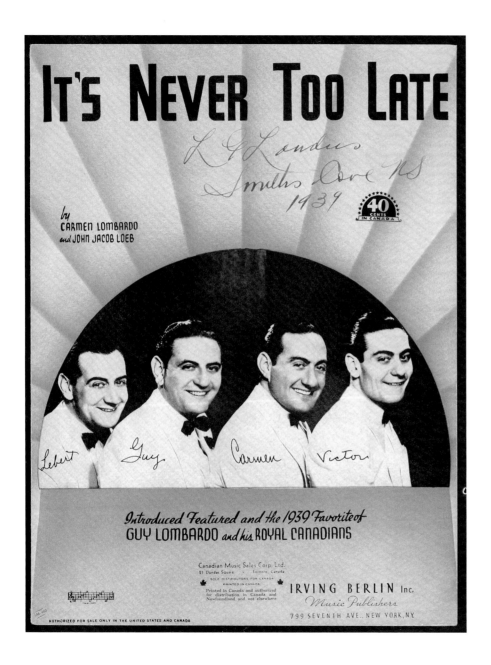

"My mother and my Aunt Laura were immigrants, to London, in Canada, but they married cousins from Cleveland. They had to, there was nobody else Jewish in London. Or almost nobody. So every two weeks, religiously, if I can put it that way, all summer, we would get ourselves over to the Ninth Street Pier and take the boat across to Port Stanley, and the relatives would come down from London and we'd have a picnic on the beach and spend the day swimming and gossiping. That was in the late twenties. I still miss it."
—Honnie Busch, Cleveland

Around the same time, an Italian immigrant couple in London was having a similar problem. They had four marriageable sons, all making their way as musicians in a family band, but there weren't a lot of eligible Italian girls for them to choose from. These boys, too, took the ferry across the lake, and two of them found wives there. They also found prosperity. *AC*

For many Ontarians, the notion of embarking on one of the glamorous excursion boats was as farfetched as a quick trip on a space shuttle would be for their descendants. This was still an overwhelmingly rural society. New inventions like sewing machines and combines were making life a bit easier, but farm families still worked from dawn until dusk, fishermen had no time for holidays during the ice-free months, and loggers cut trees until well after the snow fell. Everybody turned out at picking time. Whole families are on the job in this 1890s picture of hops harvesters on a farm near Leamington. *WT*

Harvesting the barley, Fisherville, 1906. Ontario barley had been an important crop since the mid-nineteenth century, when American brewers discovered its pleasingly delicate color and flavor. *AO*

A small dry dock at Port Stanley, 1923. The big shipyards were on the other side, but every port had its scaled-down version. Here, the *Morgan*, a fish tug owned by Charles and Thomas Morgan, is getting a refitting. *NAC*

Laying track for a spur line north of Port Burwell, 1895. *NAC*

Winter brought new chores. Cutting and maneuvering large blocks of ice up a ramp and onto a sleigh bound for the community ice house was tough going, but at least you could be sure the supply would never run out. These Port Stanley men are working a short way up Kettle Creek, c. 1910. *Courtesy of Frank and Nancy Prothero*

Another kind of ice cutting. After a 1918 storm, Captain George Irwin, the Port Colborne lighthouse keeper, arrived one morning to find his place of work covered in ice two feet thick. A conscientious man, he spent the day chopping his way back in while his wife recorded the event. *Courtesy of Marian Grimes*

Attempting to cross the frozen lake on foot seems a foolhardy adventure, and most of those who have tried it were acting strictly out of necessity—soldiers marching under military orders, the occasional sailor whose boat had become trapped in ice and who had to hike to safety, escaping slaves, or criminals fleeing the law. But a few have undertaken the challenge "just because it was there." The fellow in this 1947 photo has started out on a mid-winter stroll from Ashtabula to visit friends on the north shore. *PDHM*

When work was finally done, there was time to enjoy the scenery. Here, the Backus family—Sarah, John Henry, and John C., of Port Rowan, bask in the beauty of the lake's Carolinian woods in 1885. The large, bushy-haired dog sitting in one of the middle chairs is actually the family's pet bear. *LPCA*

The Waddle family of Port Dover enjoys a lakeside picnic with a few friends, c. 1890. *PDHM*

Drawing, embroidering, quilting, rug hooking, decoy carving, fashioning twig furniture and other homespun crafts provided an outlet during long winter evenings. In some families it seemed as if everyone could draw or paint or whittle. Captain Alexander McNeilledge was not only a skilled cartographer but also a self-taught artist who worked fanciful, accurately rendered drawings of sailing ships into his maps.
NHS/EBDM

Hayrides were a high spot of small-town social life. The wagon in this 1910 Port Dover photo seems to have more people on board than hay, but that isn't preventing anyone from having a great time. Port Dover was fortunate in having attracted a number of superb photographers over the years; this picture was taken by Toronto writer/photographer M. O. Hammond, who often summered on the lake. *AO*

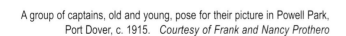

A group of captains, old and young, pose for their picture in Powell Park, Port Dover, c. 1915. *Courtesy of Frank and Nancy Prothero*

The hauling of a gigantic pine down the main street of Port Dover in 1890 brought out the photographers. The tree was so big that there was no other way of getting it down to the sawmill. *NHS/EBDM*

The tradition of north shore eccentricity found a new and fascinating exemplar with the appearance of Hiram Walker. Born poor in Massachusetts in 1816, he went west to Michigan in the 1830s and eventually took up the manufacture of fine whiskey. Leery of the growing American temperance movement, in 1859 he set up new production facilities across the river, on land he'd purchased just outside Windsor. There, he produced a line of high-quality whiskeys that made him enormously wealthy. *Walkerville Times*

Hiram Walker barrel makers and bottlers. *WT*

Like many self-made Victorians, Walker was something of a megalomaniac. He named his headquarters Walkerville, and after the death of his wife, Mary, he built an Anglican church and designated it St. Mary's. To facilitate the delivery of hops, Walker put in a railway line to Kingsville, on Lake Erie. Then, because he wanted to live in Detroit, he created his own ferry line across the river. He also supervised the building of an entire small city to house his workers. But like Thomas Talbot he preferred his people docile; anyone who declined to live where assigned was out of a job. On the other hand, Walker had a progressive side and had been deeply influenced by utopian building schemes such as the English Garden City movement. He took a chance by hiring a young, visionary German-American architect, Albert Kahn, to design his personal domain and encouraged him as he created block after blaock of innovative, charming buildings. Every street had a distictive feel, and the beautifully designed parks were open to all Walker's employees. *WT*

The firm's head office, modeled on the early sixteenth-century Palazzo Pandolfini in Florence. After Hiram died in 1899, his heirs, while retaining his architectural vision, quickly discarded his social ideals. Albert Kahn, a Jew, would not have been allowed to live in the buildings he had designed. Nor would other kinds of "undesirables," such as non-whites. Fortunately, the bigotry is long gone, while many of the original structures remain. *WT*

The outbreak of the Great War. While the isolationist Americans stayed out of it, hundreds of thousands of Canadian boys cheerfully signed up to fight and frequently die for King and Empire. The three-year hiatus before the Yanks joined in, when Canadian eyes were focused almost exclusively on the events in Europe, saw the further transition of Canada from a far-flung collection of settlements to a psychologically coherent nation. This unusual photograph was taken in the Amherstburg station in early 1915 by one of the recruits on his way toward the trenches in France. Their spirits were probably high, but the faces of the families and friends they were leaving behind tell a different story. *PC/FMHS*

PATRIOTIC
MOONLIGHT EXCURSION

Thursday Evg, July 20
8 TO 10.30 P.M.
FARE FOR ROUND TRIP 25c.

TWO HOURS' RIDE ON LAKE ERIE

The Young Ladies' KHAKI CLUB have arranged for a delightful "Outing" on the palatial steamer **"PELEE"**

Proceeds to be devoted to "Convalescent Home for Canadian Soldiers"

Music supplied by the Celebrated Citizens Band. Refreshments---The girls will make this a special feature. Dancing---In order not to offend anyone, there will be no dancing. Married Men---Come, bring your wife and family. Single Men---Come, bring your girl. Girls without fellows---come and we will furnish a fellow. Fellows without girls, ditto. Everybody come and help make the excursion a "Humdinger."

This poster is issued by MR. WM. T. GREGORY, Hon. President of the Khaki Club, who assumes all responsibility for its phraseology.

P. S.---It is confidently expected that all business places will be closed for this excursion.

GOD SAVE THE KING.

On the home front, women's groups organized quilting bees and lake excursions to raise money for the war effort. This voyage out of Leamington was sponsored by a group known as the Khaki Club ("proceeds to the Convalescent Home for Canadian Soldiers"). In true rural Ontario style, the poster promises a humdinger of a good time on the palatial steamer *Pelee*, while making it clear that in order not to offend anyone, dancing will be strictly forbidden. *NAC*

The steamer *Pelee* in the 1950s, a bit worse for wear. *AO*

Food producers along the lake did what they could for the war effort. This apple evaporator plant at Port Rowan provided hundreds of thousands of dried apples for the boys in the trenches, whether they wanted them or not. *NHS/EBDM*

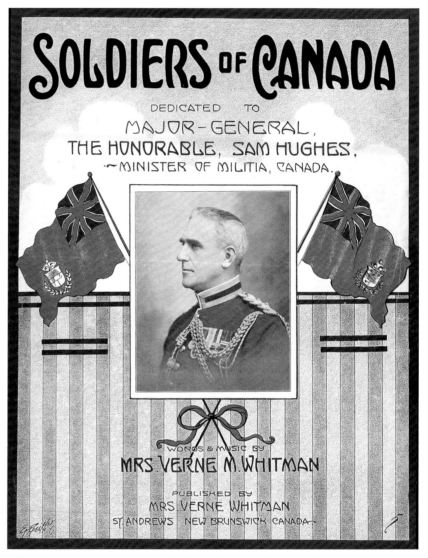

"Everybody wants ta get inta the act," as Jimmy Durante used to put it. "Everybody," in this case, included manufacturers who did their best to link themselves to the war effort and dowagers who published patriotic songs about the boys overseas. "We pray thee, God of Power and Might/Be with our boys, Canadian boys/Oh help them at the battle's front/ to bear the brunt/to bear the brunt/ . . . " Mrs. Whitman's song was published in New Brunswick, distributed from Montreal, and purchased in southwestern Ontario. *NHS/EBDM, AC*

With the war over, life gradually returned to normal. It's harvest time on the W. H. Mitchell farm near Wheatley, 1924. *NAC*

Increasingly, truck farming was a major part of the economy. Many towns sponsored yearly tomato festivals, and orchards covered the land from the Niagara Peninsula to the Detroit River. In 1909, a Heinz ketchup plant was erected in Leamington, the first building of what was to become a huge complex. In its day, the plant was the tallest wooden building in the world, or so they insisted in Leamington.
Courtesy of Dennis Jackson

A small quantity of oil and a lot of natural gas were found under the lake. This early (1905) natural gas well was sunk near Fisherville. Today, parts of the lake bed are honeycombed with pipelines. *AO*

In 1919, another new industry appeared overnight. Prohibition was voted in on one side of Lake Erie, and the other was only too happy to help alleviate its effects. Economic historians estimate that in the Windsor–Chatham–Leamington corridor one third of the working population was directly involved in the manufacturing and shipping of illicit alcohol across the border, and that in the peak years of the mid-twenties, one hundred and fifty thousand cases of Canadian liquor crossed the Detroit River every month. This unsavory looking trio has just loaded up their car at the Hiram Walker plant for a run down to one of the hundreds of small docks along the shoreline, c. 1925. For larger shipments, the company utilized their rail network to deliver countless trainloads of liquor to Kingsville and Leamington, where it would be sent on to the Ohio markets. *WT*

The *City of Dresden*, docked at Windsor, 1886. At the beginning of its career, the wooden propeller steamer plied a regular passenger route between Windsor and the western Lake Erie ports. Almost four decades later, on November 17, 1922, the now elderly vessel left the Welland Canal at Port Colborne on a different kind of voyage. According to its manifest, it was bound for "Cuba" (better known as Detroit), carrying 1,000 cases and 500 kegs of Corby's Best, along with an undetermined amount of Old Crow. Caught in a gale, the ship foundered and broke up off Long Point. Most of the crew was saved, but the cargo came loose and began floating in toward shore. A temperance act had recently curtailed alcoholic consumption in Ontario, so as word of the bonanza spread, the population of nearby Port Rowan made a mad dash for the shoreline. The lookout at the lifesaving station was the first to spot the incoming contraband and scored 40 cases all by himself. The rest of the cargo vanished over the next two days. Only then did someone get around to notifying the authorities, and not a single bottle of whiskey was ever officially recovered. *PC/FMNS*

As dusk fell, armadas of heavily laden motor launches headed out across the lake. Port Colborne boasted a regular fleet of twenty boats, and no doubt a fair number of irregulars as well. During one twenty-five-day period in 1927, a full 7,000 bottles of ale, 86 cases of wine, 60 cases of gin and 2,070 cases of whiskey left that port for Buffalo. The *Grey Ghost*, seen here in 1926 in Port Dover, was a typical rum-runner. Painted a dull grey, these low-slung boats were virtually invisible once out on the lake. *HCGL*

Organized crime was closely linked to prohibition in the U.S., and Canadian editorialists threatened dire consequences as a result of Canada's enthusiastic acquiescence in the liquor trade. No one took them too seriously. In any case, prohibition profits began to dwindle in the late 1920s when the Coast Guard added powerful new patrol boats to its Great Lakes fleet. With the arrival of the Depression and one in five Canadians dependent on the government for survival, the roar of the roaring twenties was soon reduced to a whimper. *MTRL*

To the Boys of H.M.C.S. Port Colborne, my very best wishes always—Sincerely, Alexis Smith

When hostilities once more broke out in Europe, the Empire again went to war first. During the First World War, women had served as volunteer nurses and held down jobs in munitions plants. Now they were putting on trousers and carrying their lunch buckets to the production line in great numbers. In this 1943 photo of a Fleet Aircraft production line in Fort Erie, all the home-front elements make their appearance—management and military brass looking on, assembly line workers, and, center stage, a competent-looking young woman machining oil ports and other small holes into a manifold. *AO*

The world was changing, and on both sides of the lake people were looking around for new ways to support the war effort. When the crew of the *HMCS Port Colborne* voted Canadian Alexis Smith their favorite Hollywood star, she obliged by sending a photo with the inscription: "To the boys of the *HMCS Port Colborne*, my very best wishes always—Sincerely, Alexis Smith." *PCHMM*

CAUTION!!

COLORED PEOPLE

OF BOSTON, ONE & ALL,

You are hereby respectfully CAUTIONED and advised, to avoid conversing with the

Watchmen and Police Officers of Boston,

For since the recent ORDER OF THE MAYOR & ALDERMEN, they are empowered to act as

KIDNAPPERS

AND

Slave Catchers,

And they have already been actually employed in KIDNAPPING, CATCHING, AND KEEPING SLAVES. Therefore, if you value your LIBERTY, and the *Welfare of the Fugitives* among you, *Shun* them in every possible manner, as so many *HOUNDS* on the track of the most unfortunate of your race.

Keep a Sharp Look Out for KIDNAPPERS, and have TOP EYE open.

APRIL 24, 1851.

Warnings like this were often posted in northern cities. This example from Boston is one of the few still in existence.
The Freedom Seekers

Chapter Five

REFUGE ON THE OTHER SIDE

When neighboring countries share a common language and things are going smoothly, it's easy to forget that each jurisdiction has its own distinct laws and outlooks. But during more turbulent eras, a principle that seems obvious and unarguable in one place may appear unfair, even immoral, just down the road, or just across a stretch of water; in extreme cases, when all else has failed, a dash for the nearest border seems the only way out.

In Lake Erie's history, the refugees from perceived injustice fleeing across the water have at times been Americans, in other periods Canadian. The first flow of refugees began even before the Revolutionary War had officially ended, as the defeat of the British turned thousands of Loyalists into outcasts within their communities. The late eighteenth century was a time of intense political debate and upheaval, and feelings ran high on all sides for many years. President Washington, who loathed Tories, denounced the families who fled to Canada as "unhappy wretches, deluded mortals," and John Graves Simcoe, when he was lieutenant governor of Upper Canada in the 1790s, referred to Americans as "a rapacious, ambitious people."

The Edisons of New Jersey, mentioned earlier, were one of those refugee families. After first living in Nova Scotia, they

Samuel Edison Jr., late in life. *Edison Museum of Vienna*

Samuel Jr.'s son, Thomas Alva, was born in Milan, Ohio, in 1847. Although his father chose not to return to Canada, young Tom paid regular visits to his grandparents' farm. He learned to swim in the creek there, and his first job away from home was night telegrapher for the Grand Trunk Railway near Stratford. But he was too ambitious to settle in rural Ontario. This June 16, 1888, picture shows Edison collapsed at a table after seventy-two straight hours of intense struggle with an improved version of his wax cylinder phonograph. *EMV*

a lieutenant in a local rebel detachment. Once the ill-fated uprising was crushed, Thomas Talbot ordered his personal goon squad to teach those disgraceful ingrates a lesson. At the Edison farm, Samuel Jr.'s quick-thinking stepmother delayed the thugs long enough for him to slip away. Young Sam fled across the province, then slid and stumbled his way over frozen Lake St. Clair to safety in the Michigan Territory. Eventually, he drifted back to Lake Erie, ending up in the river town of Milan, just upstream from Sandusky, Ohio.

Of all the asylum seekers who have crossed Lake Erie, none have been as desperate as African-American slaves fleeing north along the Underground Railroad. As one Stephen Foster-influenced lyric of the era put it: "I am on my way to Canada, that cold and distant land/The dire effect of slavery I can no longer stand/Farewell, old master, don't come after me/I am on my way to Canada, where coloured men are free." John Graves Simcoe had taken steps to abolish slavery in Ontario during his term as lieutenant governor in the 1790s and the first escapees headed north soon afterwards, even though the practice persisted to a small degree. When in 1833 slavery was officially banished throughout the British Empire, that initial trickle became a steady stream. Exactly how many runaway slaves actually crossed the border is unclear. Fifty years ago scholars were agreed on about seventy-five thousand; however, the next generation of historians debunked that figure and declared that the number was thirty thousand at most. Today, the estimate is back up again. Whatever their numbers, the majority of escapees settled in Ontario.

They said, "Is this Canada?" I said, "Yes, there are no slaves in this country." They seemed to be transformed . . . they laughed and cried, prayed and sang praises, fell upon the ground and kissed it, crying "Bless the Lord! I'm free before I die!" From the 1860 log of a Buffalo-bound Lake Erie captain. He had picked up two fugitives in Cleveland and let them off at a secluded Ontario beach.

eventually settled on a farm outside Port Burwell in the Talbot Settlement. For them, as with many others along Erie's north shore, being able to claim descent from a Loyalist family became a badge of honor. When the War of 1812 started, Samuel Edison Sr., was one of the first to take up arms against the Americans, and as a captain in the First Middlesex Regiment was present at the surrender of Detroit to Brock and Tecumseh.

By the 1830s, the political landscape was becoming more complicated and the Edisons were again in the thick of things. Samuel Jr. also took up arms, but for a very different cause than his Loyalist father. The young Edison fell under the spell of William Lyon Mackenzie's fiery anti-Family Compact rhetoric and became

As usual, Edison's hard work paid off. His phonograph proved particularly useful for alleviating the loneliness of rural life. After Edison's death in 1933, Henry Ford, who had always idolized the inventor, bought up the Ontario homestead lock, stock, and barrel—furnishings, stones, and even trees. He then transported this piece of rural Canadiana to his American history corral at Greenfield Village, near Detroit. *AO*

Many of the escape routes led through Ohio, which had a long common border with the slave states of Kentucky and Virginia (there was no West Virginia at this time) and was traversed by numerous north-south rivers and canals. Travel by water was considered safer than by land. *Historical Atlas of Ohio*

As the Underground Railroad expanded, Oberlin, Ohio, just inland from Lorain, became a central distribution point. In 1858, the town became the scene of a national cause celebre when slave catchers tracked down an eighteen-year-old escapee. Townspeople, along with students and professors at Oberlin College, armed themselves and freed the youth, but their leaders were arrested, The Oberlin Twenty, as they became known, spent three months in the Cleveland jail. *OCA*

The Oberlin Rescuers
At Cuyahoga Co. jail April 1859

1 J. R. Shepard.   5 W. Evans.   9 S. Bushnell.   13 A. W. Lyman.   17 J. Watson.
2 O. S. B. Wall.   6 E. Boyce.   10 J. Scott.   14 J. Bartlett.   18 J. M. Fitch.
3 L. Wadsworth.   7 R. Plumb.   11 M. Gillett.   15 W. E. Lincoln. 19 H. E. Peck.
4 D. Watson.   8 H. Evans.   12 C. Langston.   16 R. Winsor.   20 D. Williams.

118

OUT·JAIL!

THE RESCUERS

Are coming TO-NIGHT !

At a public Meeting at the Mayor's Office it was voted that the citizens, en masse, turn out to meet them at the CARS, and escort them to the Church for Public Reception. The undersigned were appointed a Committee of Arrangements:

H. L. HENRY,   A. N. BEECHER,   W. P. HARRIS.
J. M. ELLIS,   E. R. STILES.

The committee appointed Father Keep for President of the Meeting at the church, and **Prof. J. M. Ellis, Marshall.** All the citizens are invited to meet the Rescuers at the Depot at half-past seven. The procession will form after the Band in the following order:

The Mayor and Council; The Fire Department in Uniform; The Rescuers; The Citizens.

Let there be a grand gathering !

Oberlin, July 6.   **By order of Committee of Arrangements.**

A celebration was held when the rescuers returned to Oberlin. *OCA*

The *Arrow* doubled as an abolitionist vessel. During its regular Sandusky–Detroit run, the passenger steamer often made unscheduled stops at Malden (Amherstburg) to drop off escapees. *UWO*

Not surprisingly, many of the ex-slaves became farmers in Canada. This 1921 photo was taken at a North Buxton farm owned by descendants of escapees. The ex-slave settlement near Chatham, in the extreme southwest of Ontario, also became a busy lumbering center with its own rail line to the lake. Getting acclimated to the frigid weather was another story, and every winter many died from "northern" diseases like pneumonia. *Buxton National Historic Site and Museum*

North Buxton was founded in 1849 by William King, a fiery Irish minister. Reverend King believed in education and more education; at his school Latin and Greek were required subjects, and graduates often went on to do brilliantly in university. When local white families caught on to what was happening, so many chose to transfer their children to North Buxton that the local county school closed for lack of students. This 1910 photo shows teacher George Cromwell surrounded by students. *BNHSM*

Isaac Riley, born into slavery in Missouri, had escaped to Canada with his family. While working in St. Catharine's, he got wind of something that sounded too good to be true—someone down near Windsor was offering ex-slaves both cheap land and free education. Riley, determined that his four children would be educated, led the family on a 300-mile walk across the province. The talk proved to be more than rumor; he received a 50-acre parcel of land at $2.50 an acre (payment deferred for ten years), and his children were enrolled in the school. Today Riley's portrait hangs in the North Buxton Museum as an inspiration to his descendants. *BNHSM*

Clarissa Johnson's mother was a house slave for a New Orleans family. Every summer the family went north to Ohio to visit relatives, and at age twelve she was taken along to mind the children. Her mother instructed Clarissa to run away once they crossed the Ohio River. She was to travel north by night until she found someone she could trust to help her get to a place called Canada. The young girl successfully eluded the slave catchers and somehow found her way to North Buxton, where she eventually married and raised several children. She never again heard any news of her mother, nor did her family ever know what had happened to her. *BNHSM*

North Buxton's small downtown displayed a certain atypical insouciance. There weren't many communities in southwestern Ontario where you were likely to come upon a combination gas station, post office and community center called Papa Prince's Pleasure Parlor. *BNHSM*

122

Emancipation Day Parade, Amherstburg, 1894. In the years preceding the Civil War, an estimated ten percent of the town's population consisted of former slaves. They were the impetus behind the holiday, which was first celebrated on August 1, 1834, a year to the day after slavery in the British Empire had been officially abolished. While many ex-slaves returned south after the war, a large enough number stayed on to mount a yearly parade. Afterwards, everyone went on a picnic, and in the evening a grand ball was held. In many Ontario cities the tradition continued on into the 1970s. *NAC*

Near the mouth of Ohio's Sandusky Bay lies a low, unprepossessing chunk of land known as Johnson's Island. During the Civil War, the site housed a notorious prison for Confederate officers. If Johnson's Island was not quite the hellhole of southern prison camps like Andersonville (these were officers, after all), it was bad enough. Food and warm clothing were in short supply, medical treatment was virtually non-existent, and though the barracks look solid enough in this 1863 photo, they had been hurriedly built of green wood. During the freezing winter of 1863–64, when the temperature dropped to –26 Fahrenheit, the prisoners would waken covered in snow that had blown through gaps in the warped boards. Of the ten thousand prisoners who passed through the gates, a substantial proportion never left. *HCGL*

RICHMOND WALKER

JOHN BELL STEELE

The dashing Richmond Walker was one of the lucky ones. After the war he returned to his native Mississippi, where he died in 1909. Of John Bell Steele nothing is known beyond this *carte de visite*. He may have gone home to his wife, or he may be buried in a common grave somewhere on the windswept island. By the time the citizens of Sandusky got around to building a proper cemetery in 1890, most of the records had long since vanished. *FH/SL, FH/SL*

The border and freedom lay a few scant miles away, and the prisoners spent much of their time contriving escape strategies. (Canada at this point was something like Switzerland in the First World War; southern sympathizers, spies and *agents provocateur* used it as a base for creating confusion in the Union states.) In September of 1864, with the connivance of friends in Ohio, prisoners conceived a plan to send a band of civilian sympathizers, posing as passengers, to take over the excursion steamer *Philo Parsons*. The steamer would then approach the unsuspecting Union gunboat guarding the island and overwhelm its crew. Running up to Johnson Island, the two boats would take on as many prisoners as possible before the Yankee guards realized what was going on, then the vessels would cross the lake and be run aground on the Canadian shore. The plan should have succeeded; the conspirators even managed to commandeer an extra ship, the *Island Queen* (the Sandusky– Toledo ferry is seen here in an 1860 photo). But an alert officer on the gunboat sensed something was up, and when he apprehended the ringleader the carefully hatched plot collapsed. Its leaders were sentenced to death by hanging, although in the end only one was executed. During the entire sad history of the Johnson Island prison, only three men successfully escaped and made their way to Canada. *Lore of the Lakes*

A hundred years passes before another cross-lake refugee story comes to notice. The Edison family is involved once more, this time through an eccentric grandniece of Thomas Alva Edison. Inspired by the pseudo-medieval illustration on a tin of Turret cigarettes, in 1929 she built a castellated house (at one point it even had a moat) in the picturesque cliffside village of Port Bruce and lived there until her death. Fittingly, for the past many years the castle has been the home of a war resister who crossed the border to Canada during the Vietnam War. *AC, AC*

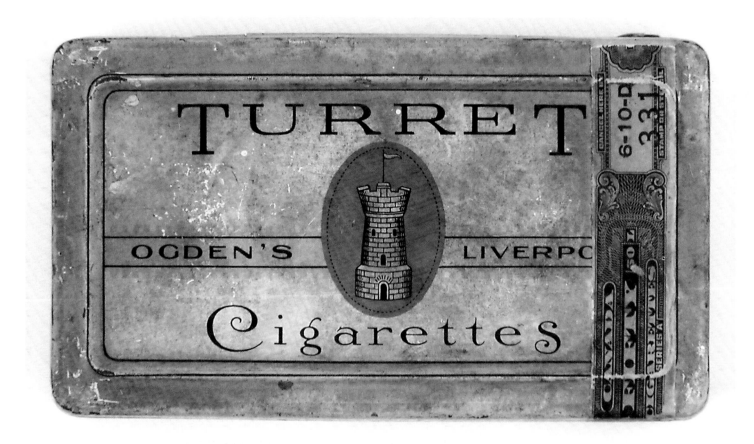

Chapter Six

THE HIGH INDUSTRIAL REVOLUTION, 1880-1945

By mid-nineteenth century the American lake ports were abuzz with commercial wheeling and dealing, but doubts were beginning to creep in. Things were happening too fast. Which of the multitude of new inventions and manufacturing processes people read about in their morning paper would prosper? Which would vanish overnight? Where should their hard-earned money be invested? Would the railroads put paid to lake shipping? Was the real action now taking place farther west? Could it all have been merely a pipe dream? The bank failures and panic of 1857 seemed briefly to confirm people's fears.

There were also increasing intimations of war, frightening on a personal level but at the same time traditionally a boost to a sluggish economy. Supplying the Union army in the impending Civil War would call for vast quantities of iron and steel—not to mention food, transport, housing and everything else a modern army required. Sure enough, by the time Robert E. Lee surrendered his sword at Appomattox the cities on Lake Erie had built up an enormous manufacturing base and were on their way to even greater prosperity.

As the century drew to a close, the great metropolises had pretty well sorted themselves out. Cleveland would specialize in shipping,

Two boys walk their dog on the Cleveland waterfront, 1888. *HCGL*

The main Westinghouse plant in Cleveland, c. 1900. *CPL*

general manufacturing, and iron and steel. Toledo, just off Maumee Bay, was a center for glass production and a major rail and shipping hub. Buffalo had solidified its position as the most important lumber, grain and livestock distributor east of Chicago. Detroit, already a center of rail-related manufacturing, was, courtesy of Henry Ford, about to add a brand-new industry that would revolutionize modern life. Not that any city had a monopoly on its specialties—cars were produced in Toledo and Cleveland, ships in Buffalo, glass in Detroit, iron and steel everywhere. There were more than enough customers to go around.

The men in this 1918 photo appear at first glance to be playing in a brass band, but a "glass band" might be a closer description of Libbey's master glassblowers at their craft. The barrels on the floor, known as bit buckets, hold water used in cooling down the glass. The row of pegs above the men are cooling ducts, a primitive but essential form of air conditioning for employees working with open flame. *Libbey Glass*

The lake remained the lifeblood of smaller communities. Ashtabula, Lorain and Sandusky, all with fine harbors, did best, but between shipping, shipbuilding, and the growing commercial fishery it was almost impossible for towns on the south shore of Erie not to prosper. The nation was impressed by this Midwestern dynamism; of the eleven presidents elected between 1868 and 1920, seven (Grant, Hayes, Garfield, Harrison, McKinley, Taft and Harding) were from Ohio. Another Ohioan, William Tecumseh Sherman, would have been a shoo-in had he not famously refused either to run if selected or serve if elected.

Lake Erie's tycoons, during what became known as the Gilded Age, had more money than they knew what to do with, and it was all theirs. Income tax would not come into existence until the 1920s. So these men spent, and spent, and spent. Their first step was to build themselves sumptuous palaces that trumpeted their

success to the world. One stretch of Cleveland's Euclid Avenue, known as Millionaires' Row, was lined for seventy-five blocks with the massive mansions of newly rich industrialists and bankers. The orgy of conspicuous consumption came to a grand finale at University Circle, where an ornate public garden presented to the city by Jeptha Wade provided a backdrop for the upper crust to show off their latest finery. When domestic design no longer inspired them, the potentates hired celebrated architects to design new company headquarters. Then, to further express the heights to which they had risen, they dabbled in the arts. Some, to their credit, became deeply involved and endowed not just museums but libraries, theaters, concert halls, university buildings, civic gardens and zoos. A few founded universities; Wells College in New York State owes its existence to Henry Wells of Wells, Fargo and Cleveland's Case Institute of Technology was founded by industrialist Leonard Case. The new millionaires also built up art collections to stock their museums, and after dark dutifully sat with their wives in theater boxes while the civic orchestras they had helped fund played Mozart and Beethoven.

In 1920, Cleveland, with a population of nearly a million, ranked as the sixth largest city in America. Buffalo checked in at just under six hundred thousand inhabitants, and Toledo at about half that number. In the excitement of the extended economic boom, it sometimes seemed as if everyone was getting rich; in reality, for every industrialist and financier there were a thousand ordinary Joes and Josephines laboring in offices and factories and corner stores without much hope of moving higher up the economic ladder.

Many of them were newcomers. The rush of immigration from northern Europe had just begun to dissipate when whole villages in places like Sicily, Poland, Russia and Rumania began packing up their belongings and heading for America. Between 1880 and 1920 an estimated twenty-five million immigrants from southern and eastern Europe arrived on American shores. A large number of these refugees from economic deprivation and ethnic prejudice found their way to the booming cities of the Great Lakes.

Near the end of the First World War, the United States unleashed its industrial might against Germany. Afterwards, however, the country retreated back into isolationism, and when the Second World War broke out in 1939 America again remained a non-participant for the first few years. It took the surprise attack at Pearl Harbor in December of 1941 and Hitler's subsequent declaration of war in support of Japan to shock the U.S. into joining the struggle.

Neither increasing industrialization nor war's alarums and excursions had much effect on one part of Lake Erie—the secluded archipelago of small islands that hiphops across the western basin between Point Pelee, Ontario, and Sandusky, Ohio. The largest of these, Pelee Island, is Canadian, as are the tiny bits of land named North Harbour, Hen and Chickens, and the three Sister Islands.

In American waters, Kelleys Island, North Bass, Middle Bass and South Bass support small year-round populations. Ohio State University maintains a teaching laboratory on Gibraltar Island, just off South Bass, and though the Johnson's Island prison is long gone, cottagers are said to share the place with a Confederate ghost. The miniscule pieces of real estate named Mouse, Green, Ballast, Gull, Rattlesnake, Sugar, and Starve islands are visited only by the birds.

But in its early days the archipelago was witness to its share of history. Perry fought the Battle of Lake Erie just off South Bass, Pelee Island was the scene of a significant skirmish during the 1837 rebellion, escaping slaves hid out on the islands while finding their way north on the Underground Railroad, and bootleggers once slipped unobtrusively through the narrow channels as they transferred their contraband cargo to the States.

At the turn of the twentieth century, rail traffic dominated transportation. A job on the railroad seemed to be a guarantee of lifelong employment, and you didn't even have to wait for pay — the money came to you. In this c. 1900 picture, a pay car on the Pittsburgh and Lake Erie Line has just arrived at a substation, and the workers are boisterously lining up to receive their week's wages. *NAC*

The speed and scope of economic expansion in the early years of the twentieth century was staggering. A typical example is the career of an obscure Cleveland inventor, Joseph Duncan. In 1902, his American Multigraph Company was working out of a cramped, one-story building on a back street. Twenty-five years later, after perfecting a new process capable of handling thousands of pieces an hour, the firm's headquarters had expanded to fill the entire square block, and Addressograph-Multigraph had become a world leader in an industry that hadn't even existed thirty years earlier. *CPL*

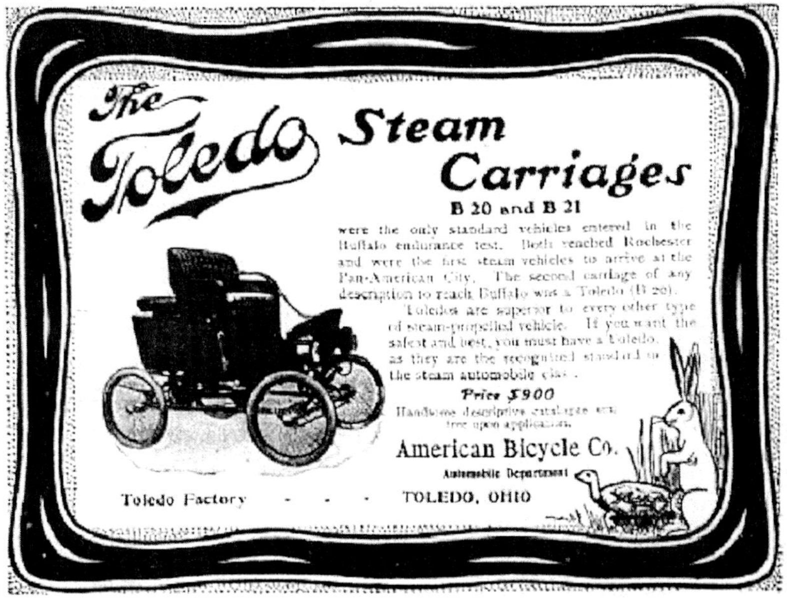
The Toledo Steam Carriages
B 20 and B 21
were the only standard vehicles entered in the Buffalo endurance test. Both reached Rochester and were the first steam vehicles to arrive at the Pan-American City. The second carriage of any description to reach Buffalo was a Toledo (B 20).
If you want the safest and best, you must have a Toledo.
the steam automobile class.
Price $900
American Bicycle Co.
Automobile Department
Toledo Factory - - - TOLEDO, OHIO

Up in Detroit, Henry Ford was turning out inexpensive automobiles for the masses with his name on them. His motto was, "A Motor for the Multitude." A rival company in Ohio went after the same market, declaring in a 1904 issue of *McClure's Magazine* that "if you want the safest and best, you must have a Toledo." And all for only nine-hundred dollars. Not that the upper classes were neglected; that same year the Pope Motor Company was offering its mile-a-minute luxury version of the Toledo, which would set you back a mere thirty-five hundred dollars. *McClure's Magazine*

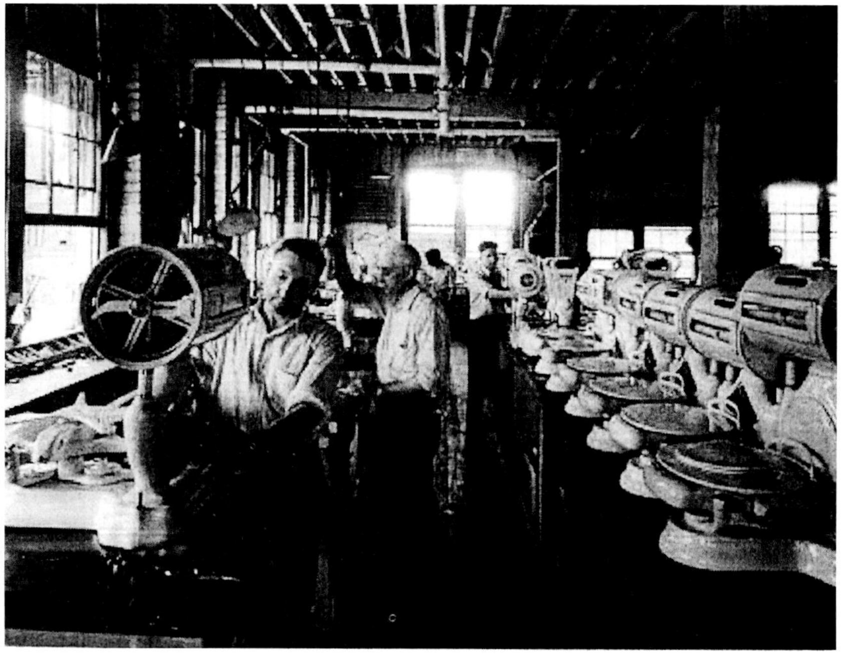

The Toledo Scale Company, founded in 1900, became one of that city's best-known manufacturers. *Toledo's Attic*

As the century advanced, continuous expansion was creating jobs galore, and more and more women were beginning to apply for them. Sometimes, notably in the garment trade, that meant putting up with long hours and appalling working conditions, but these Sherwin-Williams stenographers, c. 1905, look comfortable enough at their desks. An early version of the dictaphone takes up a large portion of each woman's work space. *SW*

Hulett unloaders at work, c. 1930. George Hulett's design for huge hydraulic lifters was the equivalent of inventing the wheel for Lake Erie shippers. The Cleveland engineer's device was first tried out at Conneaut in 1898, where one of his monstrous machines unloaded 5,250 tons of iron ore in under four hours, a job that would have taken days using manual labor. Within a few years every Great Lakes shipper of any size had converted to this type of unloader. *AC*

The American Shipbuilding Company, based in Lorain, Ohio, was founded in 1898 as a consortium of Erie ship builders. With additional yards in Cleveland and Toledo, ASB came to dominate Great Lakes shipbuilding and soon was one of the top three yards in the nation. This photo shows the gala 1899 launching of the steel-hulled *Superior City*, the first modern long-line ore carrier. The fact that the hatches had been designed to coordinate with the new Hulett unloader, itself in use for only a year, is one indication of how quickly new ideas were put into production. *Black River Historical Society*

By 1916, the Cleveland yards of the American Shipbuilding Company took up as much space as the entire commercial waterfront had a few years earlier. *HCGL*

A group of ASB draftsmen hard at work planning the future in the Lorain yard, c. 1900. *BRHS*

Port Clinton, Ohio, waterfront, c. 1890. Workmen in the small ports had to be jacks of all maritime trades. This scene includes a shipyard, two fish plants, numerous warehouses, a small grain elevator, a cannery, a lift bridge and several piers. *HCGL*

Huron Harbor, c. 1905. This small Ohio town began life as a French trading post in the 1700s, disappeared for several generations, then resurfaced as a lake port specializing in black coal and red ore. *GLHC*

Like Huron, Ashtabula, was a leading coal port. With a fine harbor and an excellent location, the city rapidly expanded into an important port, capable of handling large freighters such as those shown in this early twentieth-century picture. *HCGL*

Ashtabula's Center Street, c. 1900. It's no accident that the two store signs that can be made out are outside pool halls; Ashtabula's success as a maritime center had a down side. At night, the sidewalks teemed with hundreds of unruly sailors looking for a good time, in whatever form they could find, and the town had long since taken over Long Point's reputation as the toughest locale on the lake. Even today you can meet older women who recall their mothers making them promise never to go downtown after dark. *HGCL*

Spanish-American War Victory Parade, Cleveland, 1898. To their surprise, in 1898 Americans found themselves involved in a foreign war, with Spain as the unwilling enemy. "Remember the *Maine!*" cried the jingoists after the giant steamer sank in Havana Harbor. Men like Ohio senator Marcus Hanna, who had made a fortune in shipbuilding and steel and was now combining the two with the arrival of steel-hulled ships, looked forward to a profitable conflict. But the barely seaworthy Spanish navy was destroyed so swiftly that the shipyards never were called on to take up their tools. *CPL*

Not everything came up roses, of course, even in boom times. On August 3, 1915, nature gave the terrified citizens of Erie a reminder of how capricious she could be. A series of powerful thunderstorms dropped 5.4 inches of precipitation on the city in less than six hours. Millcreek, which normally drifted placidly through the downtown area, became a raging river. One of the cross-town culverts became blocked, creating an ever-rising reservoir four blocks square. Suddenly, the culvert gave way, releasing millions of gallons of debris-strewn water. The torrent destroyed everything in its path. Thirty-six people drowned and 313 structures, including the house in this picture, were demolished. Property damage came to two million dollars. Still, at least one sharp cookie found a way to make a buck from the disaster. This photograph is actually the front side of a picture postcard, sent from a small town near Erie a little more than a month after the storm. *AC*

Buffalo's neo-classical Albright Art Museum, just after it opened in 1902. The museum (now the Albright-Knox) was named for its major contributor, steel magnate John J. Albright. The white marble façade was impressive on its own, but the collections in its vaulted, pillared halls were even better. *WNYH*

John D. Rockefeller's summer cottage in Forest Hill, a bucolic tract of parkland at Cleveland's eastern edge. When fall arrived, the city's most prominent citizen would return to his stately mansion on Millionaires Row. In 1884, Rockefeller decided he needed more scope than Cleveland could offer and decamped to New York, but his wife insisted on returning every summer for a few weeks of Midwestern peace and tranquility. *AC*

Lafayette Square, Buffalo, c. 1910. Buffalo boasted the most beautifully laid out of the Lake Erie downtowns; its wide avenues and perfectly designed squares gave the city an architectural élan and an aesthetic completeness few North American cities could match. *WNYH*

Guarantee Building, Buffalo. Louis Sullivan's Guarantee Trust building, an early skyscraper built in Buffalo in 1895, is acknowledged as one of the great masterpieces of American architecture. H. H. Richardson and Frank Lloyd Wright, the two other outstanding American architects of that era, also designed buildings for the Queen City. *LC*

141

Ellicott Square, Buffalo, 1900. The splendid Ellicott Building was the largest office building in the world when it was built in 1896. The square seems oddly empty of vehicles, but this was before the advent of the automobile. Hitching up the horse and buggy took a lot of effort, and unless there was a good reason, the pony usually stayed in the stable. *LC*

The boathouse in Toledo's Riverside Park, 1909. Smaller than Cleveland, less progressive than Buffalo, Toledo still had its own share of philanthropic development and visionary planning. The riverfront parks along the Maumee beat anything the larger cities had to offer in that department. *LC*

The C. B. Hall family, or at least the male side, smiles for the camera at Presque Isle Park in Erie, Pennsylvania, 1908. Erieites were lucky to have one of the few really good beaches on the south shore. The park's name, even if misspelled, was a rare remaining sign of the early French presence in that part of the world. *C. B. Hall Collection, ECHS*

In 1914, one hundred thousand Clevelanders showed up to watch this amateur championship baseball game between Telling's Strollers and Hanna's Cleaners. The crowd at Brookside Park was the largest ever to attend an American sporting event, although the record lasted only until the next year's final game. In 1915, no less than one hundred and fifteen thousand fans, a number equal to twelve percent of the city's population, filled the hillsides. *LC*

AMATEUR CHAMPIONSHIP GAME
STROLLERS VS HANNA'S CLEANERS
BROOKSIDE STADIUM — SEPT. 20, 1914.
ATTENDANCE 100,000

COPYRIGHT 1914
BY
The Miller Studio
2205 CLARK AVE
CLEVELAND O.

The ice wagon arrives on Cleveland's east side, 1910, to the delight of neighborhood boys and girls. *CPL*

Buffalo's Polish Market, 1906. The new immigrants brought many of their old customs. Every city of any size had its Polish section, where you could buy delicacies unheard of in most American homes. *AO*

The tenors and baritones of the Men's Jewish Singing Society of Cleveland pose for a photo in 1911. Choral groups, drama societies and dance troupes could be found in all the ethnic neighborhoods. *CPL*

A street fair in the Italian quarter, Buffalo, 1906. *AO*

Buffalo tenements, c. 1930. With no unions to speak of, no minimum wage and no labor codes, the vast fortunes of the industrial barons were frequently amassed at the expense of the working man. These crumbling canal district tenements, probably erected in the 1880s, housed Buffalo workers until 1936. *WNYH*

Ashtabula, c. 1908. Smaller cities had their slums, too. The residents of these Ashtabula apartments lived in the shadow of the Ashtabula Worsted Mills that employed them. There was no escaping the noise, smoke and soot, but at least they had steady jobs. *HCGL*

Brown Bomber Car Service, Buffalo, 1940. External immigration began to slow in the 1920s, just about the same time that southern laborers, both African-American and white, were moving north in large numbers looking for jobs, and along with them, more equal treatment. Race soon became a difficult issue in all the northern cities. Calling a cab in a black neighborhood, for example, was seldom a simple matter of picking up the receiver. Local businesses, such as the Brown Bomber Car Service, which borrowed its name from heavyweight champ Joe Louis, soon arose to provide local services. Louis, born in Alabama but raised in Detroit, was himself one of those southern immigrants to the Lake Erie region. *AC*

If you lost your job, or couldn't work because of illness, or your budget would not stretch far enough to make the rent, this shanty town on the Cleveland waterfront might be your new home. This picture dates from 1911. *CPL*

The glory days of expansion finally crashed to a halt with the Great Depression. Images of jobless men and hungry families are familiar to everyone; this 1936 photo of a young boy sitting on the steps of a Buffalo tenement can stand for them all. With one third of the nation, in Roosevelt's words, "ill housed, ill clothed, and ill fed," the good times in the lake ports suddenly seemed far away. *WNYH*

Air raid drill in a Cleveland school, 1942. Now, for the first time since the War of 1812, America found her own territory coming under threat of attack. Warnings about sabotage went up in post offices and air raid precautions became a fact of daily life. These sober-looking children are practicing taking shelter in the school basement. *CPL*

A group of Cleveland nurses boards a train in 1942 for the first leg of a long journey to Australia, where they will serve in the medical corps. *CPL*

Production lines at factories like Curtiss-Wright in Buffalo, which had been producing civilian aircraft, now assembled jeeps, tanks and fighter planes. *WNYH*

ASB yards, Lorain. During the First World War, ASB shipyards had turned out more than two hundred freighters for the cause. But that impressive figure was dwarfed by the new war effort. The ASB yard in Lorain churned out mine sweepers, corvettes and destroyers. Cleveland contributed numerous tugs and lighters, and a Toledo shipyard came up with a revolutionary new twin-propeller icebreaker, the Mackinaw. In this photo, taken December 29, 1943, Corvette Hull #844 is being launched at the Lorain yards. By the time the Axis powers surrendered in 1945, the vast mountains of military material produced by American factories had surpassed anything the world had ever seen. *BRHS*

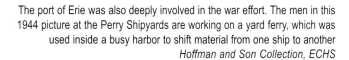

The port of Erie was also deeply involved in the war effort. The men in this 1944 picture at the Perry Shipyards are working on a yard ferry, which was used inside a busy harbor to shift material from one ship to another
Hoffman and Son Collection, ECHS

Grape handlers at the Pelee Island Winery, 1900. Galinée had exclaimed in his 1669 diary about "les raisins sauvages" (wild grapes), which he and Dollier found growing in great profusion along the lakeshore. "We made wine of them with which M. Dollier said Holy Mass all winter, and it was as good as vin de Grave." Two centuries later, early settlers on the islands followed his cue; by 1878 there were seventy-one commercial wineries on South Bass Island alone, Andrew Wehrle's Golden Eagle Winery on Middle Bass was the largest wine producer in the United States, and Pelee Island had become the site of Canada's first commercial vineyards. *Pelee Island Winery*

The popular Wein Stube, or wine bar, at the Lonz Winery on Middle Bass, c. 1910. *HCGL*

The Bay View winery was located on Kelleys Island. *HCGL*

When the leading citizens of the great cities took a break from empire building, they often headed for the islands. The fabulously wealthy banker Jay Cooke ("the man who financed the Civil War") bought Gibraltar Island and erected a stone mansion on a bluff, in which to spend his summers. In the late 1880s a local entrepreneur created the palatial Hotel Victory not far away on South Bass. The Victory featured eight hundred rooms, a 600-foot verandah, and a ballroom with a twenty-three-piece orchestra. Advertisements promised romance in abundance, with caves to explore, secluded paths to hike, beaches, boating, and non-stop entertainment. Unfortunately, the builders overreached themselves and in 1892 the Victory went bankrupt. After the derelict building finally burned to the ground in 1919 (the flames could be seen in Detroit, 35 miles away), Put-in-Bay took over as the islands' main tourist center, but nothing ever matched the mad opulence of the Victory in its brief heyday. *LEIHS*

Winters on the islands are long and lonely, but for the few brave souls who stay on year-round there are compensations. These ice yachts (left to right: *Maud S, Gypsy, Icicle, White Wings, Snowbird, Haze, Cyclone, Mildred, Arctic, OT Sears,* and *North Wind*) are sailing off South Bass in 1890. *HCGL*

The Middle Bass volunteer fire brigade, 1909. For people living in wooden houses on an isolated and windy island, fire is always a danger, as the Victory Hotel's fate so graphically proved. This photo was taken just after the brigade had successfully doused a house fire. *HCGL*

Yet another fall storm sweeps into Port Dover. *NHS/EBDM*

Chapter Seven

STORMS AND SHIPWRECKS, FIRE AND ICE

At last we arrived . . . at the shore of Lake Erie," Pere Gallinée recorded in 1669, "which appeared to us at first like a great sea because there was a great south wind blowing at the time. There is perhaps no lake in the whole country in which the waves rise so high." A later visitor, Oliver Hazard Perry, grumbled politely to William Henry Harrison about conducting a war that depended on the whim of the climate: "The weather begins to be Squally, and disagreeable, and we can hardly Calculate from one hour to another how the weather is to be. I know Sir, you will cross the moment you are ready . . . In great haste/I am D Sir/With great Respect/your Obd. Servt/O H Perry." And Harrison, when criticized by a journalist, pouted to Perry in turn, "I dare say the writer would have been unwilling to have hurled himself in a frail open boat in one of the Storms to which he says Lake Erie is Subject."

And so it went. Indian agent Thomas McKenney noted in 1816: "Lake Erie. . . is a vast sea, and often more stormy and even dangerous than the ocean itself." On his 1842 tour, Charles Dickens found travel by water not that much more comfortable than by land. "It's all very fine talking about Lake Erie," he railed, "but it won't do for persons who are liable to seasickness . . . it's almost as bad as the Atlantic. The waves are very short and horribly constant."

We leaves Detroit behind us
We sets our canvas tight,
The tug slows up and casts us off,
Old Erie heaves in sight.

So we watch our tiller closer,
We keeps our sheet ropes clear,
There's no such thing as a steady wind
Along Lake Erie here.

1890 song

Collisions were another danger. Most took place in bad weather or at night. In 1847, the sidewheeler *Chesapeake* was struck by a schooner, the *John A. Porter*, because the latter's helmsman mistook the lights on a third boat for shore lights. Both boats sank, with loss of life. Sometimes the lake was so crowded that vessels collided in broad daylight, as when the *Despatch*, a coasting vessel stationed at the Port Maitland naval depot, rammed the steamer *Commerce* on a clear day. An entire regiment of Royal Welsh Fusiliers were on board the *Commerce*, on their way to London with their families; twenty-three soldiers and thirteen family members were drowned in that 1850 disaster. Charges were brought against both captains.

Competing weather fronts—warm, moist air from the south and north winds swooping down across Canada—frequently clash over the lakes, resulting in sudden, fierce storms. Add in the fact that Erie's shallowness guarantees viciously choppy waves, and you've got the recipe for marine disaster, particularly in the days before ship-to-shore radio, scientific weather forecasting, foghorns and lighted buoys. The lake bottom is littered with thousands of wrecks, although not all are as well preserved as this one. *Courtesy of Rob Cromwell*

Of all the hazards a captain might encounter, nothing compared with a real Lake Erie storm. Anything could happen then and any sensible captain, once he realized what was coming, would head for port as fast as possible. Of course, a storm could blow up without warning, as many unfortunate mariners learned to their dismay, and when that happened reporters and headline writers often outdid themselves in hyperbole. The front page of the Erie *Daily Times* of September 13, 1900, for example, blared:

AWFUL NIGHT OUT ON WATER
MANY NARROW ESCAPES FROM DISASTER
ALL CAPTAINS REPORT HIGHEST SEAS EVER

But "highest seas ever" is a relative phrase. Here's a tally from the Kingston *Chronicle* of a severe November gale back in 1820:

The schr. *Franklin*, Capt. Hayt, of Erie . . . with a cargo of between three and four thousand dollars worth of merchandise, belonging to Mr. Hamot . . . sailed from Erie and arrived at Grand River. The capt. went on shore, but returned to his vessel when the gale came on. The schooner now lies sunk in about five fathoms of water . . . the tops of her masts just above the water, 10 miles below Grand River. The crew are lost—consisting of Capt. Hayt, and a Mr. Norton, pilot, and two others, all of Erie, Pa.

The schr. *Zephyr*, Napier master, from Ashtabula to Sandusky, with a quantity of goods and salt, was driven on shore near the Pennsylvania and Ohio line, with the loss of every soul on board — amounting to 10 or 12 persons, the crew and passengers. The body of a female was found on the shore.

Another small craft is said to be lost, but we have no particulars.

The schooner *Elizabeth*, of U. C. is reported to be lost, with most of her crew.

That 1820 blow sounds bad enough, but when Lake Erie salts settle down to shoot the breeze three more recent storms invariably dominate the conversation. All took place in the late fall, in 1913, 1916 and 1940, and people are still arguing about which one truly deserves the title "storm of the century." For the Great Lakes as a whole, a storm that began on Friday, November 7, 1913, generally gets the nod as the most fearsome. Captains from Duluth to Kingston were caught unprepared by the sudden, ferocious blizzard. During the six-day blow, which downed telegraph lines and left the entire city of Cleveland in the dark, some lucky crews made it into the nearest safe harbor. Others tied themselves to the rigging or just kept bailing and somehow survived. But the final count showed that 249 men lost their lives in the storm. Their frozen bodies continued to wash ashore for days, some still wearing soggy, ice-encrusted life preservers.

Storms are one thing. A warm, calm spring day, an experienced captain and crew, and a relatively new vessel equipped with every modern device should be proof against unexpected events. That's what Captain Slackford of the sandsucker *Kelley Island* might have said. (A sandsucker is a kissing cousin to a dredger, except that after being collected from the lake bottom the sand is transported to shore for sale. Until fairly recently sand was an essential industrial product, used for many construction tasks, including as a sound barrier between floors.) But sandsuckers are tricky vessels to maneuver, and this was Lake Erie, where you can never be sure of anything.

A gruesome tale . . .
9 sailors die off Point Pelee as sand barge tips
-Captain William G. Slackford, Sandusky
-his son, William, the cook
-seven others, including a deckhand . . . known to the crew only
   as 'Tommy'
           (headlines in the *Border Cities Star*, May 4, 1928)

The crew of the 200-foot-long, 35-foot-beam *Kelley Island* had anchored 3 miles south of Point Pelee, lowered a chute 35 feet down to the lake bed, and spent the afternoon suctioning up sand. When the hold was full they began hoisting the chute using a crane. Just as they were finishing, an unexpected wave crashed over the side, driving the men back. Water poured in through the open hatch, the heavy crane tipped ominously, the load of sand shifted, and the vessel began to turn turtle.

I was in my bunk at the time . . . When I heard the whistle I guessed what was wrong and I slid right out of my pants, kicked off my shoes, and in my BVDs beat it from the stokehold to the deck. There I saw she was foundering. The captain was still in the pilot house and still pulling that whistle. I tried to get the lifeboat but only had time to cast loose a rope. She started to roll and I grabbed the side, but

when she finally heaved over I was thrown clear.
        Scottie Petherbridge's account,
          as reported in the *Border Cities Star*

As Petherbridge told it, the heroic captain continued to pull the whistle "until the very pilot house was in the water." The crew of the fish tug *Flossie G.* noticed the sandsucker in trouble, but by the time they got there only seven survivers could be found clinging to the wreckage.

Very early on it became obvious that mariners needed help in navigating the treacherous lake channels. Lighthouses were the first line of defense, although not always the most permanent. Standing alone and exposed, the tall structures took a constant beating from the wind and waves, and their foundations, no matter how thick, were occasionally undermined by the shifting sands. The port of Buffalo has gone through nine different beacons (ten if you count a lightship once anchored in the harbor) since the first 60-foot lighthouse went up in 1818 at the mouth of Buffalo Creek. That one was soon replaced, not as a result of construction defects, but because its beam was too weak to penetrate the haze from the city's wood-burning stoves.

This anchor had lain undiscovered for 102 years when it was dredged up in Ashtabula Harbor in 1939. *NAC*

A Lake Erie waterspout is a kind of water-skimming mini-cyclone.
A quick-witted and obviously rather intrepid artist by the name of
William A. Johnson sketched this 1838 example as it swept by.
MTRL

When winds are high, even the rivers entering the lake
may be affected for miles upstream, as these bobbing
vessels on the Detroit River demonstrate.
PC/FMHS

A 1929 photo of the storm-bound *William H. Truesdale* taken by the freighter's chief engineer as he clung to a lifeline leading from the aft deck to the bridge. *Great Lakes Historical Society*

The prevailing westerly winds erode the low cliffs lining much of the northern shore and drop their sandy deposits farther east. In the process, the shoreline is constantly refigured, and the many sand bars and sand points often shift without notice. No wonder Lake Erie captains get gray hair. *NHS/EBDM*

When the wind and the barometric pressure combine in a certain way, the lake can drop as much as 15 feet at one end and rise by an equal amount at the other. On October 18, 1844, a substantial portion of the water in Buffalo Harbor suddenly sloshed ashore, destroying homes and businesses for ten blocks inland and drowning a large number of innocent bystanders. This undated photo of a storm surge at Port Maitland gives a hint of the lake's destructive capacity. *DDHA*

Only nine years after the 1841 burning of the *Erie*, the sidewheeler *GP Griffith* set off from Buffalo carrying 326 passengers and crew. Most of the former were immigrants from Germany and Ireland. Within sight of Cleveland, a small fire broke out on an upper deck. There seemed little danger, but before they could make port the ship stuck on a sand bar. Perhaps under the illusion that the shore was closer than it looked, a few passengers began swimming toward the shore, a mile away. The rest soon followed. The next morning 154 bodies were found washed up on the shore. According to local legend, many wore heavy money belts containing their life savings in silver and gold and were dragged under when they refused to release them. *HCGL*

165

At least once, a sand point played a part in saving lives instead of ending them. On July 20, 1907, four young Port Ryerse girls were sedately canoeing along the wooded shoreline of Long Point Bay when a sudden gale pushed them out into the lake. Each new gust drove them farther from shore. With the swell increasing moment by moment, the Four Brave Girls (as they would come to be known) kept their wits about them. Two paddled furiously while the others bailed with their petticoats, but to no avail. They were headed for certain death in open water when their boat miraculously caught on sand at the outermost curve of Long Point. As the exhausted girls struggled through the rough surf toward the beach, they heard a furious barking. The lighthouse keeper, alerted by his dog, appeared over a dune and came to their rescue. Today, this painting of the event by local artist Edgar Cantelon hangs in the Port Dover Museum. (A contemporary of the girls, he got the scene right, as in his original the teenagers were alone on the stormy sea. Those erratically proportioned vessels in the background were added a few years later by one of Cantelon's rivals.) *PDHM*

After their rescue, the girls (left to right: Edna Stickney, Louella Winter, Louise Howick and Stella Howick) posed for a formal portrait in the Gordon Photographic Studio. Their story was widely reported, and the Four Brave Girls joined Abigail Becker as heroines of Long Point. *NHS/EBDM*

A sudden freeze-up in the late fall of 1926 has trapped this fleet of freighters in the western basin. All they can do now is wait for the arrival of an ice-breaker or hope for a thaw or a heavy wind to break up the ice.
NAC

Given Erie's northern latitude, it's not surprising that the lake has had its share of mini-*Titanics*. On April 14, 1936, the open-prowed fish tug *Wilma* was struck a violent blow on her starboard side by a large chunk of ice. Despite the crew's efforts to stop up the gaping hole with blankets, the vessel began to list. Another boat was close enough to rescue the men, but within minutes the *Wilma* had plunged to the lake bottom (where it remains today in 76 feet of water, a popular site for Port Dover recreational divers).
Courtesy of Rob Cromwell

The *American Eagle*, built in Sandusky in 1880 by John Monk, helped extend winter travel around the Lake Erie islands. Her much-admired white oak hull could break through 24-inch blue ice. Converted to a tugboat in 1901, she burned at Toledo seven years later, but her name lives on in the western basin's American Eagle shoal, where she once got stuck. *UWO*

Getting stuck in the ice was a frightening, not to mention humiliating, prospect for any lake captain. In 1928, the *Altawandron*, a tug belonging to Captain John Matthews, became ice-bound 18 miles southwest of Long Point. The boat soon ran out of supplies, but rather than abandon ship, Captain Matthews and crewman Les Murphy trekked 20 miles across the frozen lake to Port Rowan where they bought seventeen dollars worth of groceries before heading back. After ten days, the wind shifted enough to clear a path and the crew returned to Port Dover to find the docks lined with cheering family members. *PDHM*

At first glance, this faded photo of the *Collingwood* at a Port Colborne pier seems to have little significance. But there's a date on it — November 9, 1913 — which makes it the only known photograph taken during the great Armistice Day storm. A momentary lull appears to have allowed the crew to spend a few moments ridding the vessel of the tons of heavy ice formed over the previous two days. *PCHMM*

The *James B. Colgate*, c. 1915. "Black Friday," October 20, 1916, hit Erie hardest of the five lakes. Forty-nine lives were lost when three large freighters and one schooner were caught out on the water in 70-mile-an-hour winds. The giant Cleveland-based steamer *Merida* sank off Wheatley, Ontario, with all twenty-three men (the wheelhouse was later found at Port Stanley, 60 miles east). A lumber hooker, the *Marshall F. Butters*, ran into waves so high they put out the fire in the boiler. The hooker's whistle could not be heard over the howl of the wind, but a nearby ship spotted puffs of steam coming from the spout and rescued the crew. The Canadian schooner barge *DL Filer* began taking on water near Bar Point, off Amherstburg, and Captain Mattison instructed the crew to climb the rigging and hold on for dear life. He then watched in horror as the mast cracked under their weight and pitched the men into the raging waters. When the whaleback steamer *James B. Colgate* foundered off Long Point, most of the men in this picture went down with the ship. *HCGL*

GLHS

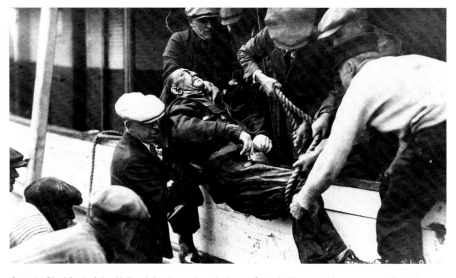

Captain Slackford of the *Kelley Island* wasn't as lucky as Captain Keenan. Here crewmen from the *Flossie G.* grimly retrieve his lifeless body. *PC/PPNP*

Captain Keenan sits for a formal portrait with the tools of his trade, his sextant and pelarus, 1870. Lake captain was a prestigious, highly skilled occupation, and the men who had reached that station in life were in no doubt of their importance. Keenan worked out of Buffalo and when ashore made his home in Fenwick, Ontario. *PCHMM*

The rescuers stand glumly on the inverted hull of the *Kelley Island*, no more survivors left to find. The boat was later raised and rebuilt. *PC/PPNP*

The busy port of Ashtabula got its first lighthouse in 1835. *HCGL*

This evocative, 50-foot square-rigged lighthouse, seen through the mists of a thick Lake Erie fog, has stood in the harbor of Lorain, Ohio, since 1917. *Black River Historical Society*

As far back as the 1820s the ubiquitous Captain McNeilledge was pointing out the dangers of Point Abino, where a rocky shelf extends out from the Canadian shore just west of Buffalo. (Albino was originally Aveneau, after an early Jesuit visitor.) Under pressure from the Americans, the somewhat dilatory Canadian government finally anchored a lightship there, only to have it vanish in the great storm of 1913. So when this unique and elegant seven story Queen Anne structure was finally erected in 1918, lake captains cheered. *Courtesy of Kevin Harding*

The Long Point Rescue Team. In 1883, Canada's Federal Ministry of Marine and Fisheries established a lifesaving station at Long Point. During the shipping season the wooden structure, which had a 25-foot observation tower, was manned round the clock by a captain and a crew of seven. Their self-righting, double-hulled boat, seen here on a practice run c. 1920, could skim the waves at 10 miles an hour. The captain acted as coxswain. *NAC*

The design of lifesaving stations is pretty much the same the world over. The station in Fairport, Ohio, seen here c. 1905, was a typical Lake Erie version. The lifeboat, resting on a flatbed carrier, was launched by rolling it down a track from the boathouse into the water. The whole procedure, from the crew piling aboard to heading out to sea, could be managed in a matter of seconds. *HCGL*

The freighter *CW Elphicke*, carrying 160,000 bushels of flax, ran aground on a lee shore off Long Point on October 21, 1913. A close look at the picture reveals that the ship's back is broken. The crew was plucked off by the Long Point rescue boat shortly before the ship broke in two. *NHS/EBDM*

175

Point Pelee got its lifesaving station in 1902. The first director, Lewis Wilkinson, is credited with saving a total of 376 lives during his twenty-six-year tenure. After he retired, the new boss, Captain James Grubb, proved his worth when a major gale blew in on October 24, 1929. Grubb received word that the *NJ Nessen*, a Detroit cargo steamer packed with lumber, had run aground off Leamington. The thirteen crew members were visible from shore as they clung desperately to the rigging. Thinking fast, Grubb ordered his rescue boat and crew loaded into a truck and driven to a point on the shore closest to the stricken vessel. In this newspaper photo, the rescue team has unloaded its boat and is about to put out toward the *Nessen*, which can be seen in the upper right. "I never felt more thankful in my life, than when I saw that lifeboat," the captain of the *Nessen* said later. "I didn't think it would be possible . . . to get through those breakers to us." It was a good thing they did make it; the Nessen broke up shortly afterward. *PC/PPNP*

(Blessed Be the Fountain)

...than the snow; ... ... whit-er than the snow; ... Wash me in the blood of the Lamb, ... And I shall be whit-er than snow. ... of the Lamb, ... than snow.

23   Brightly Beams Our Father's Mercy

P. P. B.   (Lower Lights)   P. P. Bliss

1. Bright-ly beams our Fa-ther's mer-cy From His light-house ev-er-more,
2. Dark the night of sin has set-tled, Loud the an-gry bil-lows roar;
3. Trim your fee-ble lamp, my broth-er: Some poor sail-or tem-pest-tossed,

But to us He gives the keep-ing Of the lights a-long the shore.
Ea-ger eyes are watch-ing, long-ing, For the lights a-long the shore.
Try-ing now to make the har-bor, In the dark-ness may be lost.

D.S.—Some poor faint-ing, struggling sea-man You may res-cue, you may save.

CHORUS
Let the low-er lights be burn-ing! Send a gleam a-cross the wave!

Back in 1870, a popular American preacher named Dwight Moody was on board a schooner bound for Cleveland when a gale blew up. The worried captain and crew, not sure how far they were from their destination, peered into the dark night for lights on the shoreline to help guide them, but their eyes met only blackness. Fortunately, this was one vessel that eventually made its way to safety, but Moody's imagination kept replaying those frightening moments out on the lake. Next Sunday morning his sermon text was "Brethren, the Master will take care of the great lighthouse; let us keep the lower lights burning." Sitting in one of the pews that morning happened to be a writer of popular hymns, Philip Bliss. Listening to Moody develop his theme, he began working over his own idea for a new composition. "Brightly Beams Our Father's Mercy" became a gospel standard and can still be found in hymnals today. *AC*

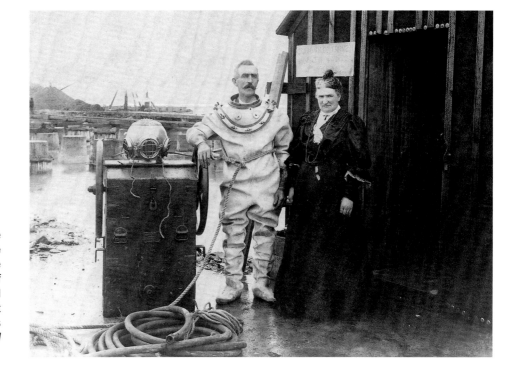

Divers have long made attempts to explore the countless wrecks on the lake floor. The first workable diving suit was designed in 1839. Pioneer Lake Erie diver Johnny Green described what it was like back in those days. "The pressure was immense. The rush of blood to the head caused sparks of various hues to flash before my eyes, and I had a constant tendency to fall asleep." Half a century later, the diving equipment still looked somewhat dubious. This 1895 picture of a government diver identified only as "Mr. Fraser, with Mrs. Fraser" was taken in Port Colborne. *PCHMM*

Chapter Eight

FUN ON THE LAKE

Recreation, in the days before jet travel and freeways, used to be pretty much a local affair. That was fine if you were lucky enough to live near Lake Erie. You could swim in its clear waters and sunbathe on its sand beaches, then when it grew dark dance the night away in one of its many lakeside ballrooms. You could also sail or canoe or try out a new-fangled speedboat, or cast a line into waters so filled with fish even the newest neophyte couldn't help catching a full pail. If putting on the style was your dish, there were cruises to the sophisticated environs of downtown Detroit or Cleveland or even Chicago. And if you wanted peace and quiet, with some nature thrown in, Canada was just the ticket.

Left: On the beach at Port Stanley, one of the big three Canadian resorts, c. 1920. These young mothers were lucky to find an uncrowded space on the sand. It must be a weekday, because on Saturday and Sunday the little resort town was jammed to the gills with ten thousand or more visitors. Holiday weekends could attract half again that number. *UWO*

Two popular resort complexes dominated the eastern end of the lake. Erie Beach, in Fort Erie, Ontario, and Crystal Beach, a few miles farther west, catered to bridge and ferry traffic from the Buffalo area, as well as Canadians from cities on the Niagara Peninsula. In this photo, the steamer *Americana*, bringing hundreds of Yankee sun lovers, is about to dock at Crystal Beach, c. 1910. *FEMB*

In 1927, the London and Port Stanley Railway, which owned much of the Port Stanley waterfront, erected the largest ballroom on the lake. The L & P S Pavilion could accommodate two thousand couples at a time. Locals referred to the barn-like structure as the "Stork Club" for its pretensions at high life. *Courtesy of Frank and Nancy Prothero*

"The band was positioned on the raised platform in the center left, while the dancers did their stuff on the floor just below. I worked there as a rope boy. That meant it was my job, mine and another kid, to clear the floor after a number finished. We'd start at one end and stretch a rope all the way across and work our way to the other end, sort of herding the dancers out the exits. See, to get back on for the next dance you had to pay again. Five cents a dance was the going price, for the house bands, anyway."

Douglas Flood, London

Members of the popular Vincent Lopez Orchestra pose on the dance hall's opening day. Duke Ellington, Count Basie, Benny Goodman, Tommy Dorsey, and other big-name bands made regular appearances. Their practice was to fit Port Stanley in on a weekday, between shows in the major cities. If, for example, the Ellington Orchestra had a gig in Buffalo on Sunday and another in Detroit or Cleveland on Wednesday, an easy way for Duke to pick up some spare change was to break the trip with a stop in Port Stanley. Besides, everyone liked the place. The musicians could let down their hair and have some fun, too. When one of the top bands came to the Stork Club, ticket prices rose all the way to twenty-five or fifty cents. *UWO*

Benny Goodman soaks up some rays outside the Stork Club in the summer of 1936. With him is local bandleader Morgan Thomas. *Courtesy of Hilda Deak*

Benny Goodman swings—and misses—as he warms up for an afternoon game between his orchestra and the Morgan Thomas cats. Goodman was a better clarinetist than ball player, but it was his team, so he always got to play. *Courtesy of Hilda Deak*

181

A few daring visitors to Port Stanley ride the erector-set Ferris wheel on the grounds of another dance hall, the Stanley Beach Casino, c. 1910. This small, early structure is remembered as the place where Guy Lombardo and his brothers got their start as the house band. *Courtesy of Frank and Nancy Prothero*

Happy Crowds Praise Casino

London dance devotees are afforded a rendezvous worthy of Palm Beach, at the spacious, beautiful CASINO, PORT STANLEY. The remodelled, enlarged and greatly-improved building has amazed and gladdened thousands of dance enthusiasts who have already inspected and admired the many new features planned for your approval.

Lombardo's *Famed Orchestra Plays Every Evening.*

PORT STANLEY
L. & P.S. Shelter Pavilion

Thursday Evening May **12th**

ORIENT CLUB ANNUAL

DANCE

FEATURINF THE TRIUMPHANT RETURN OF LONDON'S OWN

GUY LOMBARDO and his ROYAL CANADIANS

Offering All the Big Hits of Their Cleveland Broadcasts.

2 Orchestras—McKenna's Collegians—2 Orchestras

Admission 75 Cents. Tax Extra. Special L. & P. S. Trains.
Leave London 7.20, 8.20; Lv. St. Thomas 7.45, 8.55. Returning, Lv. Port Stanley Beach 10.50, 11.30 p.m., 12.15 and 1.15 a.m.

L. & P. S. PAVILION NOW OPEN EVERY EVENING FOR DANCING
Stuart McKenna's Collegians. Standard Admissions 15c. Dancing 5c. L. & P. S. Ry. Summer Fares Every Day.

Two newspaper ads featuring Guy Lombardo. The first was inserted in the local paper by the Stanley Beach Casino in 1922, a few months before the Lombardos would take off for the bright lights of Cleveland. The second shows how their fortunes had changed in four short years across the lake. From house band at a small Ontario dance hall, the boys were now "Guy Lombardo and his Royal Canadians," and Guy's intuition that the new medium of radio represented the road to success (he was so sure about it that at first he paid for air dates out of his own pocket) put the Lombardo family band out in front of all the other dance orchestras in America. Small venues like the Stanley Beach Casino were a thing of the past. *UWO*

The dance pavilion at Crystal Beach, c. 1942. Looking at the lively crowd in this wartime photo, it's hard to believe that during the previous conflict, organizers of a fund-raising patriotic excursion had banned dancing "in order not to offend anyone." But events like this one represented the end of the line for the dance halls. Rock and roll and television were waiting in the post-war wings. *FEMB*

Located on a small Canadian island in the Detroit River, Boblo's beautifully designed amusement park and large dance hall were landmarks of Detroit life for nearly a century. *PC/FMHS*

A Boblo ferry at its berth on the Detroit waterfront, c. 1910. Anyone lucky enough to have made the trip from the Motor City's grimy downtown to bucolic Boblo Island remembers it as an idyllic outing, somewhat like voyaging to Narnia or Oz and back in the space of an afternoon. *PC/FMHS*

In its heyday, Erie Beach had it all—rides, midways, animal acts, a huge lake pool, a zoo, restaurants, a grand ballroom and pier, plus a sports stadium. The crowd in this 1920 photo are watching an intercollegiate track meet with the park's wooden roller coaster in the background. *FEMB*

Racing of every conceivable variety was wildly popular in the speed-obsessed early years of the century. In this inter-vehicular event held on the Niagara River opposite Buffalo, the speedboat jumped into the lead, but the flying boat, as it was called, passed it before the finish line. *WNYH*

A train-against-plane race near Cleveland, 1925. You can almost feel the engineer urging his train on, but we have no way of telling which mode of transportation won. *NAC*

Port Stanley, 1927. A crowd has gathered to watch a motorcycle race. Behind them are the lake, the beach, the railway tracks, a full parking lot, and the dance pavilion. The contestant in the foreground is about to start up a hill. *UWO*

Cedar Point, Ohio, situated at the end of a long sand spit, was reached by causeway or by hourly ferries from Sandusky. In addition to a splendid beach, Cedar Point boasted an eight-hundred-room art-nouveau-style hotel with a variety of card rooms, music rooms, fanciful lobbies and overhanging balconies. Every summer the popular resort hosted a long roster of athletic events and festivals. Religious ceremonies were also on the agenda; in the 1920s a mass baptism drew ten thousand sinners, eager to have their souls saved by being dipped in the waters of Lake Erie. But Cedar Point's greatest claim to fame was its selection of terrifyingly high roller coasters. Leap the Dips, erected in 1912, was one of the first. The names have changed, but even today Cedar Point's daredevil rides are hard to beat. *CPHA*

Only true daredevils took on Cedar Point's Cyclone. Debuting in 1929, it featured tight turns and unusually steep slopes, with a seven-story lift hill to start things off. *Sandusky Library*

The less adventuresome could cruise the boardwalk being pushed in a roller chair, at least in the early days. This picture was taken around 1895, when Cedar Point was just blossoming into a major attraction. *CPHA*

The alpha and omega of Lake Erie excursion boats. The *State of New York* was a small wooden-hulled steamer that sailed the Cleveland–Put-in-Bay–Toledo circuit in the mid-to-late 1800s. The imposing, ultra-ornate *City of Detroit III* came on the scene in 1912, near the end of the passenger steamer era. Here's a sample from the specifications book for construction of its interior: "The Marie Antoinette drawing room located aft on galley deck under palm court is to be finished in poplar and lathed chestnut . . . the water closets must have doors and seats of mahogany." *PC/FMHS, WT*

Despite its mahogany toilet seats, The *City of Detroit III's* reputation as the ultimate in lake luxury lasted only until the magnificent sidewheeler *Seeandbee* was launched the following year. Built for the C & B (Cleveland and Buffalo) Line, she was 485 feet long and 98.5 feet wide. Her seven decks had room for six thousand day passengers and fifteen hundred overnighters. The paddlewheels measured 33 feet in diameter, the engines produced up to 12,000 horsepower, each of the four smokestacks measured 9 feet across, and her cruising speed was 18.5 miles per hour. The 510 staterooms and 24 parlors were the last word in elegance. *HCGL*

The uncontested queen of the inland seas waits for passengers to board at her Cleveland dock in 1915. *HCGL*

Photos from a C & B sales brochure issued in the early 1930s. Though the *Seeandbee's* bread and butter remained the regular Cleveland–Buffalo round trip, the boat also advertised special cruises with a limited passenger list. These publicity shots were intended to entice young sophisticates on board for an enchanted journey to the upper lakes. The near left shows one of several art deco lounges; the other is an artfully composed shot of some gay young things playing one of the ship's many games. When the Second World War broke out, the cruise ship was purchased by the U.S. Navy, stripped of her upper works, and converted into an aircraft carrier, making her the only sidewheeling flattop in naval history. Rechristened the USS *Wolverine*, she went into service as a training vessel and some fourteen thousand airmen earned their wings on her decks. *GLHS*

Boats like the *Alton* were a less grand alternative for a day on the water. On this carefree 1907 excursion out of Sandusky, the island hopper carries as many on the roof as in the seats. *HCGL*

An early lake speedboat, c. 1910. Guy Lombardo, who became a champion racer and owner, developed his lifelong passion for speedboats on the lake in just such small craft.
NAC

On this well-appointed yacht, a group of fashionable young women from Port Dover linger at the railing while the boat's owner surveys his domain, c. 1900. His relationship to them (friend? father? something else?) is unknown, but there is no question as to who is captain of this ship.
Courtesy of Peter Knechtel

Donald McAffrey: *Oh that was the wild time right along toward 1920...Everyone was so repressed through the war that we all just went nuts.*

Sally McAffrey: *Oh, yes, all kinds of crazy dances and crazy clothes. You used to go down the street with your galoshes flapping open. That was where the 'flapper' came from.*

Donald: *Well, the term came from the bird that's out of the cage and flapping but can't yet fly. (Laughs) It came to mean a girl that was pretty reckless.*

Sally: *They flapped their galoshes anyway.* (Laughs)

From A *Short History of Ontario* by Robert Bothwell. Both McAffreys were born near Lake Erie in 1889.

The young women in this late 1920s photo could be the daughters of the women in the previous picture. But times have changed; these flappers, down from London for the day, will do their own sailing, thank you very much. And while they're at it they'll wear the latest daring outfits, roll down their stockings, and come back to shore when it suits them and not a moment before. *NAC*

Of the hundreds of early twentieth-century midway booths, fish-fry outlets, taffy stands and hot-dog dispensers along Lake Erie, only one remains in business today. Built in 1912 the Arbour is still selling foot-longs to Port Dover tourists. *Courtesy of Peter Knechtel*

Chapter Nine

FISH, BIRDS AND BUTTERFLIES

Erie has always been a fisherman's paradise. Of the 177 fresh-water fish species in Canada, 138 have been found in Lake Erie; of these, 114 are considered native to the lake. The western basin's myriad marshes, shoals and reefs, in particular, provided a perfect ichthyological nursery for dozens of species, and it's not surprising that a commercial fishery was established in Maumee Bay as early as 1815. On both sides of the border, every quiet lakeside village soon had its own small fishing fleet.

Long before Europeans arrived, the Aboriginal peoples were making good use of the lake's bounty:

> Fill a pot with Lake Erie water.
> Add 3 pickerel, 3 white bass, 1 piece sturgeon
> Toss in a venison bone or two
> A few walnuts and some purslane
> Bring to a boil and cook until done.

This circa A.D. 675 recipe for Lake Erie fish stew is based on trace remains in a pot dug up at the Peace Bridge archaeological site. "Not bad at all," was the general consensus of the Native cooking students who prepared the soup, the assorted archaeologists and the newspaper reporters who sat down to a bowl in October of 1995. Curiously, while sturgeon are now rare, pickerel (walleye) and white bass are still among the most abundant food fish in the lake.

Leita Girardin and Jen O'Neil show off a giant sturgeon caught in the Girardin Fisheries nets off Point Pelee, c. 1940. *PC/PPNP*

A day of fishing and flirting at Long Point, August 1909. *AO*

The men in this c. 1900 photo, taken at Long Point, appear to be after minnows in preparation for a day's fishing. Half a millennium earlier, the Neutrals made an annual fall trek to the same site in search of migrating schools of whitefish. After a few days the Native families would return to their villages loaded down with dried fish for winter use and trade. The nets they used back then were made from woven plant fibers. *AO*

Early French visitors to the lake complained that, in spring, the creeks entering Erie were so thick with trout that sometimes it was hard to ford them. On the other hand, no one grumbled about the ease of catching a good fish dinner. In this 1906 photo, a Selkirk, Ontario trio, following a centuries-old practice, has rigged a simple net across a trout stream just before it enters the lake. *AO*

Pound fishing (also known as pond fishing) became widespread early on. The nets were attached to long stakes, which were set into the lake or river bed and left there. The principle was the same as with lobster nets; the fish swam in easily, but were unable to find their way out. In a series of carefully detailed and labeled drawings, the noted nineteenth-century Cleveland illustrator Henry W. Elliott laid out the procedure for anyone interested in trying his or her hand: (above) Lake Erie pound net boat; (right) driving stakes for pound net boat on Lake Erie. *PDHM*

The *May Queen*, an early (1864) steam tug out of Buffalo. The earliest steam tugs were all-purpose boats. They towed barges and schooners around the harbor, went to the aid of ships in distress, carried occasional cargo, and when they had no other chores, became fishing boats. Their design offered little protection from the elements; the rudimentary superstructure on the *May Queen* resembles a couple of ice-fishing huts nailed onto a deck. *HCGL*

The *Belle* brings in the day's catch, Port Dover, c. 1895. Open-style tugs like the *Belle* were already becoming obsolete when this picture was taken. *PDHM*

Two transitional fish tugs in Port Bruce Harbor, 1895. The vessel in the foreground is the *Jim and Tom*, which had a long and varied career cruising Erie's eastern basin. *HCGL*

By the late 1920s, Lake Erie fish tugs had taken on their trademark "turtledeck" look; both foredeck and afterdeck were now completely enclosed. Looking at the new design, it's almost as if the boat designers were mimicking the look of the sleek fish their crews were seeking. *PDHM*

Three tugs belonging to Cleveland's Ranney Fish Company at anchor in Ashtabula, c. 1910. The *Ciscoe* dates to 1891. The unidentified vessel to its right, more modern in appearance, was probably built about the same time as the *Lorain* (1909), which is partially hidden behind the *Ciscoe*. The older boat's cabin is partially covered, but on the newer boats the entire afterdeck has been enclosed. The boats were also growing longer. Early examples, like the *May Queen*, measured around 30 feet in length, with a gross tonnage of 10 or 12. The *Ciscoe* has evolved to 45 feet long, 13 wide, with a gross tonnage of 15. The *Lorain* is half again as large, stretching to 68 feet in length, with a gross tonnage of 49. And, in the most dramatic change from the old days, these later boats are steel hulled. This type of Lake Erie fish tug became the style setter for small fishing boats around the world. *HCGL*

December 23, 1907. Captain Allen and his crew were taking a chance going out so late in the season, but their trip paid off. The fish are grass pike. *Courtesy of Peter Knechtel*

Accidents happen, even in port. The large sloop *Julia Larsen* has suddenly capsized at the dock in Port Dover. The *Jim and Tom* was hired to salvage her, and her crew is helping to pump out the overturned boat. *PDHM*

Sandusky, Ohio, was another hub of the early fishery, and O-Lay Brothers was one of that city's largest commercial operations. In this 1911 photo, three O-Lay employees are at work out on the lake. Surrounded by water, water everywhere, the small open vessel appears ominously exposed to the whims of the lake. *HCGL*

Professional help has arrived, in the form of a diver to investigate the *Julia Larsen's* below-water damage. As usual, a crowd of spectators takes the opportunity to smile for the birdie. The diver, however, looks distinctly glum about the whole thing. *PDHM*

A fisherman's job is never done. Cotton twine nets were useless unless kept in good repair. Here an unidentified fisherman checks for tears caused by heaving masses of fish and the corrosive effect of being immersed in water for long periods of time. *PDHM*

Pound nets had to be tarred every few months to help them withstand the action of the water. The laborious and smelly task often drew crowds of interested onlookers. This Point Pelee photo dates from the early twentieth century, but a few Lake Erie fishermen continue the practice to this day. *PC/PPNP*

O-Lay Fishery employees unload fish at the company pier, while inside the plant filleters work their way through the catch, 1910. *HCGL*

The *Racey* is one of the more storied vessels in Lake Erie's history. The sleek steam tug began life in Buffalo in 1903 as a poacher under the name *Planet*. There wasn't a boat on the lake that could catch her until she ran into the Canadian patrol vessel *Vigilant* in 1907 and was confiscated and auctioned off by the government. Renamed the *Racey* and converted into a fish tug, one of her first assignments was to hurry out to the Long Point lighthouse to pick up the Four Brave Girls after their brush with mortality. A powerful boat, well into the 1920s the *Racey* was occasionally put to work as an icebreaker before the ice got too thick. That seems to be what she's doing in this 1920s photo. She was converted to diesel power in 1950, and more recently retrofitted back to steam. Today, under the name SS *Pumper*, she takes tourists on trips around the harbor of Niagara-on-the-Lake. *PDHM*

AUGUST	LBS	HERRING	PRICE	AMOUNT
2	3,245	"	71/2c	243.37
3	140	"	"	11.50
4	780	"	"	58.50
5	1,925	"	"	134.75
6	1,445	"	"	108.37
7	1,965	"	"	147.37
9	1,465	"	"	108.75
10	1,450	"	"	50.12
11	655	"	"	106.87
12	2,625	"	"	196.87
13	1,200	"	"	90.00
14	5,600	"	"	420.00
15	8,300	"	"	622.50
16	3,510	"	"	263.25
18	15	SALMON TROUT	8c	1.20
18	20	JUMBOS	81/2c	1.70
18	1,805	HERRING	71/2c	145.35
19	20	JUMBOS	12c	2.40
19	2,010	HERRING	71/2c	150.75
20	25	JUMBOS	81/2c	2.12
20	3,515	HERRING	61/2c	163.47
21	1,000	"	"	65.00
23	980	"	"	73.50
24	945	"	"	70.42
25	2,645	"	"	171.92
27	5,425	"	7c	379.75
27	13	JUMBOS	81/2c	11.00
28	3,295	HERRING	7c	230.65
30	2,875	"	"	201.25
31	32	JUMBOS	81/2c	2.73
31	2,150	HERRING	7c	150.50

A fish tug carried a crew of six or seven. At the end of each day, the catch was weighed at the dock. The typical breakdown of a day's earnings was sixty percent to "owner and gear," forty percent divided equally between captain and crew. The captain and the owner were often the same person. A glance at the *Racey*'s fishing log for August 1920 reveals that the *Racey*'s captain was a church-going man; his boat did not go out on Sundays. Maybe he stayed home to pray for piscatorial insight, because if he and his crew were to make a decent living he had to know the fish as well as they knew themselves; weather, water temperature, migration patterns, lake depth, proximity of other boats, spawning habits and a dozen other calculations ran through his head each time he set out. August 15 was a good day; he caught 8,300 pounds of herring. The day before the catch was 5,600 pounds. On August 3, however, all the captain could manage was a measly 140 pounds, and a meager $11.50 for the entire crew to split. *PDHM*

TOTAL $4,279.05

The *Earl Bess*, out of Port Burwell, has just arrived in Sandusky during the summer of 1919. At 81 feet long, with a beam of 20 feet, the supertug was the queen of the Lake Erie fishing fleet. Her crew deserves to be recorded for posterity after hauling on board the largest one-day catch ever taken on Lake Erie— 33,000 pounds of herring. A few years later the herring fishery would collapse from overfishing. *HCGL*

Sturgeon are the Methuselahs of the fish kingdom. The species has been around for millions of years, and individual fish can live to the ripe old age of 150. A century ago, sturgeon were so bountiful that they sold for twenty-five cents each and often were not eaten but used for oil. Their numbers plummeted after people began building dikes and damming inflowing rivers, but not long ago a 186-pound monster was caught near Kelleys Island. Here a group of gutter boys at the Kolbe Fishery in Port Dover, c. 1915–20, are dwarfed by a 167-pound specimen. *PDHM*

Poaching across a watery border is an ongoing problem for any shared lake or ocean fishing grounds. Government patrol boats like the aptly named *Vigilant* had to be fast. This nemesis of numerous smugglers was built in Toronto in 1904. She ended her days quietly as a coal transport. *PC/FMHS*

A seaman poses before the drydocked *Vigilant*.
Courtesy of Harry Barrett

Smelt is one of many foreign species introduced to the lake. By the 1930s it had become a favorite food fish, not just for humans but for larger fish like walleye. During the April smelt run, as many as ten thousand fishermen would arrive at places like Long Point and Point Pelee for week-long fishing free-for-alls. So much liquor was consumed and the event became so obstreperous that eventually local residents demanded protection from the Ontario Provincial Police. Here, two Long Point fishermen hold a net full of the tasty species, c. 1950. *Ontario Ministry of Natural Resources*

Nature and the Naturalists

Earlier generations fished, dammed and trapped without much thought as to how it would all end. Not only fish, but many other animal and plant species were wiped out in the process.

The shallowest and warmest of the Great Lakes stores up heat over the summer and releases it during the winter. That's why Erie's foliage includes not just the conifers and hardwoods of the typical northern forest, but also southern species like black gum, tulip and swamp white oak. And its varied landforms—bluffs, dunes, wide beaches, clay plains, marshes, sand points and ravines dug out by the many small creeks entering the lake—all encourage a remarkable biodiversity.

Early on, the battle lines were drawn between those who saw Erie's natural bounty as a limitless exploitable resource and those who regarded it as a sacred trust. The tug-of-war tended to pit loggers, hunters and fisherman against naturalists, birders, campers and hikers; but it's never been quite that simple. The wildlife artist William Pope, for example boasted in his diary about killing and devouring 55 robins in a single day.

In his time, pioneer environmentalist Jack Miner was as celebrated a Lake Erie figure as John Maynard (a 1935 magazine poll rated Miner the fifth most famous man in America). Born in Cleveland in 1865, he came to Kingsville, Ontario, as a child, grew up to be a hunter and guide, then in 1903 underwent a Road to Damascus conversion. A flock of Canada geese he recognized as the same ones he had shot at the previous year appeared specifically to avoid the Miner property. If geese were that intelligent, he wanted no part in killing them. He turned his farm into a wildlife refuge and began lecturing on both sides of the lake about bird life. He also got the idea of attaching his address to a bird's leg before letting it go, in the faint hope that if it were killed, whoever shot it would let him know. When a letter arrived from a South Carolina hunter, it marked the beginning of bird banding in North America. Soon Miner was banding thousands of geese a year as a way of studying migration routes.

Rough-and-tumble naturalists like Miner would be surprised if they could come back and see what they had started. Erie has become the most studied lake in the world—every stretch of lakeshore, especially on the Canadian side, has its tree guy and its snake lady, its native grasses cultivator, its volunteers ready to replant or survey everything from fireflies to fish stocks. Where once there was an isolated botany professor here, a dedicated amateur lepidopterist there, hundreds (probably thousands) of trained field workers, researchers and cataloguers work fulltime trying to protect what's left of Erie's glorious natural heritage. Bird lovers scan the Internet for news of the latest rare bird sighting. Duck hunters work with wildlife groups to ensure the continuing viability of certain species. "It's about time, but probably too late, anyway," a pessimist might grump. "Better late than never," the optimist might reply.

Those last words can be applied to everything that's happened to the Lake Erie region since the Second World War. The commercial fishery is struggling, but still active. (In Canadian waters, that is. In the 1970s the U.S. banned most commercial fishing on its side in favor of sport fishing). On the north shore, tobacco is being phased out, but new crops like ginseng, exotic mushrooms and organic vegetables are replacing it. The great industrial cities, which had sunk into rust-belt obsolescence and racial chaos, are making a tentative comeback. Around the lake, smaller ports experiment with imaginative new kinds of tourism to draw people to their waterfronts. With the water cleaner than it has been for decades, the beaches are crowded, and recreational diving is increasingly popular. But Erie's overall health and the prosperity of its environs are a work in progress; it's impossible to factor in all the variables and come up with a clear prediction. For the most part, today's lake dwellers take it one day at a time, the way people always did along the shore. And on a balmy summer afternoon, with your feet dangling over the side of a small boat and a fishing rod in your hand, who would want it any other way?

Where there's fish, there's ducks. *PDHM*

Artist William Pope was among those gawking at the enormous flocks of passenger pigeons, estimated in the millions, which once darkened the skies along Lake Erie for days on end. "It is astonishing what prodigious quantities are killed and yet to all appearance their numbers are not lessened even in the slightest degree," he noted in his 1842 diary. But fifty years later the tasty game birds would become extinct in the wild; the last one being raised in captivity died in 1911. Pope made this sketch in Norfolk County during the 1830s. *NHS/EBDM*

Anna Jameson rhapsodized about the variety of flora and fauna she encountered along the lakeshore. "No one who has a single atom of imagination can travel through these forest roads of Canada without being strongly excited. The seemingly interminable line of trees before you; the boundless wilderness and the mysterious depths amid the multitudinous foliage where man has never penetrated . . . Sometimes when I looked up from the depths of foliage to the firmament I saw an eagle sailing through the air on apparently motionless wings." The gigantic nests of bald eagles were common near the lakeshore. This picture was taken near Port Ryerse. *NHS/EBDM*

A tulip tree blossom, seen in close-up beauty. *Courtesy of George E. Pond*

Every fall, endless clouds of monarchs like the ones shown here head south to Mexico for the winter. They stop along the way stop to feed on milkweed growing along the lake. *Courtesy of George E. Pond*

Fox snakes are unique to the Lake Erie region. For many years the authors shared their garage with a family of the yellowish, black-splotched creatures, which can reach a length of nearly six feet. They resemble a species of rattlesnake closely enough that they scare the daylights out of everyone the first time they are encountered. *Courtesy of George E. Pond*

A rare species of swallowtail butterfly, the spice bush swallowtail is now found only on the north shore of Lake Erie. *Courtesy of George E. Pond*

Jack Miner with one of his birds. Miner's approach was a curious mix of science and sanctimony. Not only was Miner initiating important scientific avenues of inquiry, but as a devout Christian he insisted on including a biblical passage on every bird band. In a time when science and religion were engaged in constant ill-tempered debate, Miner's "resolution" of the issue made him the darling of Bible-thumping conservatives. Three of his closest friends and leading financial donors were Henry Ford, Billy Sunday and Ty Cobb, all of them intensely reactionary and not the kind of person most men of science would choose as pals. *Courtesy of the Jack Miner Migratory Bird Foundation, Inc. / Photo by Dr. Rob Sloane*

Early sports hunters confronted by the sheer abundance of wildlife in places like Long Point and Sandusky Bay were known to go slightly kill crazy. Even the conservation-conscious Long Point millionaires were not always exempt from the mania, as is made clear in this 1880s photo of the day's kill being brought in. *NHS/EBDM*

After an 1882 trip along the lake, a young Canadian naturalist named Will Saunders raved to colleagues about the natural beauty of Point Pelee, the sandbar stretching southward toward the Erie islands. Saunders and his friends formed the Great Lakes Ornithological Club and began an intensive group study of the point's flora and fauna. In this 1905 photo, they stand in front of "The Shack," where they worked. From left to right: James Wallace, Mr. Swales, Will Saunders, Percy Taverner, Mr. Fleming. *PC/PPNP*

With the help of Oberlin College professor Lynds Jones, who also had become obsessed with Lake Erie bird life, the Ornithological club's survey led them to conclude that Point Pelee must be a stop on a major migration route. They published their first list of local birds in 1907, and it wasn't long before crowds were flocking to the point, hoping for a glimpse of the various warblers, tanagers, orioles, flycatchers, thrushes and other avian long-distance travelers. The activities of the Ornithological Club inspired others, and soon there were birders all up and down the lake. These whistling swans, which migrate each spring from the southern U.S. to the Arctic, were caught in flight by an amateur nature photographer at Turkey Point in 1920. *NHS/EBDM*

Point Pelee National Park entrance, 1918. Five years earlier, Saunders and Miner had finally gotten together; afterwards Miner wrote a glowing letter to the *Leamington Post*: "Although it rained nearly all the time I was there, yet I scarcely knew it, for I was trying to look in all directions at once, as I saw the greatest variety of trees and shrubs that stand in any one place in Ontario . . . let us combine our forces and keep Point Pelee out of the hands of unlimited wealth and preserve it for our children's children." With Miner and other supporters on board, Saunders, Taverner and their friends formed the Essex County Wildlife Protection Association, and in 1918 the group saw its efforts come to fruition with the establishment of Point Pelee National Park. *PC/PPNP*

The Franz Theodore Stone Laboratory. In 1895, a visionary Ohio State University professor established a field station for the hands-on study of the fishery's health. (It soon expanded to include all the lake's fauna.) Stone Laboratory was housed in this building on Cedar Point before being moved to Gibraltar Island, in Put-in-Bay Harbor, where it remains active. *Ohio Sea Grant/Stone Laboratory at Ohio State University*

The squawking cry of seagulls is a constant accommpaniment for anyone who lives or works along Lake Erie. On the forbiddingly named Starve Island, a Stone Lab ornithologist cradles a smaller member of the species (Bonaparte's gull or *Larus philadephia*) as he inventories birds under cover of a blind. Though this photo dates back to 1941, it could have been taken yesterday.   *(OSG/SL/OSU)*

LIST OF ARCHIVES

For the benefit of future researchers, we have compiled a list of archives with material pertaining to Lake Erie. There are many others, of course; these are just the ones we happened to find useful. AC stands for Author's Collection.

Archives of Ontario (Toronto, Ontario)
Black River Historical Society (Lorain, Ohio)
Buxton National Historic Site and Museum (North Buxton, Ontario)
Cedar Point Historical Archives (Cedar Point, Ohio)
Cleveland Public Library (Cleveland, Ohio)
Dearborn Historical Museum (Dearborn, Michigan)
Dunnville District Heritage Association (Dunnville, Ontario)
Edison Museum of Vienna (Vienna, Ontario)
Erie County Historical Society (Erie, Pennsylvania)
Follet House Library/Sandusky Library (Sandusky, Ohio)
Fort Erie Museum (Ridgeway, Ontario)
Fort Malden National Historic Site (Amherstburg, Ontario)
Great Lakes Historical Society (Vermilion, Ohio)
Hamilton Military Museum (Hamilton, Ontario)
Historical Collections of the Great Lakes/Bowling Green State University (Bowling Green, Ohio)
Historical Society of the Tonawandas (North Tonawanda, New York)
Hudson's Bay Company Archives (Winnipeg, Manitoba)
Lake Erie Islands Historical Society (Put-in-Bay, Ohio)
Libbey Glass Archives (Toledo, Ohio)
Library of Congress (Washington, D.C.)
Long Point Conservation Authority (Norfolk County, Ontario)
Metro Toronto Reference Library (Toronto, Ontario)
National Archives of Canada (Ottawa, Ontario)
Norfolk County Historical Society/Eva Brook Donly Museum (Simcoe, Ontario)
Oberlin College Archives (Oberlin, Ohio)
Ohio Sea Grant/Stone Laboratory/Ohio State University (Columbus, Ohio)
Point Pelee National Park (Leamington, Ontario)
Peterborough Centennial Museum and Archives (Peterborough, Ontario)
Port Burwell Marine Museum (Port Burwell, Ontario)
Port Colborne Historical and Marine Museum (Port Colborne, Ontario)
Port Dover Harbour Museum (Port Dover, Ontario)
Rockefeller Family Archives (Sleepy Hollow, N.Y.)
Sherwin-Williams Company Archives (Cleveland, Ohio)
Simcoe Public Library (Simcoe, Ontario)
The Jack Miner Migratory Bird Foundation, Inc.
University of Western Ontario/D. B. Weldon Library (London, Ontario)
Walkerville Times (Windsor, Ontario)
Western New York Heritage Society (Buffalo, New York)
Woodland Cultural Centre (Brantford, Ontario)

BIBLIOGRAPHY

There are a handful of books to which we found ourselves returning again and again, partly for content, partly because the writer's approach seemed close to the way we think about the lake and its history.

Burke, Thomas A. *Ohio Lands, A Short History.* Columbus, Ohio: Ohio Auditor of State, 1993.

Burns, Noel M. *Erie, the Lake that Survived.* Totowa, NJ: Rowman & Allanheld, 1985.

Cumming, W. P. et al. *The Exploration of North America. 1630–1776.* New York: G. P. Putnam's Sons, 1974.

Hatcher, Harlan. *Lake Erie.* Indianapolis and New York: Bobbs Merrill, 1945.

O'Neill, Henrietta. *In Search of a Heart.* Leamington, Ontario: Friends of Point Pelee, 1999.

Shaffer, Lynda Norene. *Native Americans before 1492.* Armonk, N.Y.: M. E. Sharpe Publishing, 1992.

Stanley, George F. G. *The War of 1812 Land Operations.* Macmillan of Canada, 1983

Wachter, Georgann and Michael. *Erie Wrecks East.* Avon Lake, Ohio: Corporate Impact, 2000.

We also found these publications helpful:

Allen, Robert S. *The Loyal Americans.* Canadian War Museum, 1983.

Allen, Robert Thomas. *The Great Lakes.* Toronto: N.S.L. Natural Science of Canada, Ltd., 1970.

Bothwell, Robert. *A Short History of Ontario.* Edmonton: Hurtig Publishers Ltd., 1986.

Bourgeois, Donald J. *The Six Nations Indian Land Claim to the Bed of the Grand River.* Ontario: Ministry of Natural Resources, 1986.

Bowen, Dana T. *Lore of the Lakes.* Daytona Beach: Bowen, 1940.

Brown, Craig, ed. *The Illustrated History of Canada.* Toronto: Lester Publishing, 1996.

Dickens, Charles. *A December Vision and other Thoughtful Writings.* Edited by Neil Philip and Victor Neuburg. New York: Continuum Publishing, 1987.

Docker, John Thornley. *Grand River Naval Depot.* Dunnville, Ontario: Dunnville District Heritage Association, 2000.

Fryer, Mary Beacock. *Volunteers & Redcoats & Raiders & Rebels.* Toronto: Dundurn Press, 1987.

Guillet, Edwin C. *The Pioneer Farmer and Backwoodsman.* Toronto: Ontario Publishing Co. Ltd., 1963 (distributed by University of Toronto Press).

Gutsche, Andrea and Cindy Bisaillon. *Mysterious Islands.* Toronto: Lynx Images, 1999.

Hatcher, Harlan, and Erich A. Walter. *A Pictorial History of the Great Lakes.* New York: Bonanza, 1963.

Hayes, Derek. *A Historical Atlas of Canada.* Vancouver: Douglas & McIntire, 2002.

Hazen, Sharon. *Down by the Bay.* Erin, Ontario: Boston Mills Press, 2000.

Henson, Josiah. *The Life of Josiah Henson.* Boston: Phelps, 1849.

Hill, Daniel G. *The Freedom Seekers.* The Book Society of Canada, 1981.

Hunt, C. W. *Booze, Boats, & Billions.* M & C, 1988.

Jameson, Anna. *Winter Studies and Summer Rambles in Canada.* New York: Wiley & Putnam, 1839.

Johnston, Charles M. *The Valley of the Six Nations.* Toronto: University of Toronto Press, 1964

Jury, Elsie McLeod. *The Neutral Indians of Southwestern Ontario.* London, Ontario: Museum of Indian Archaeology, 1982.

Leacock, Stephen. *Sunshine Sketches of a Little Town.* Toronto: McClelland & Stewart, Toronto, 1912.

Mackenzie, William Lyon. *1837: Revolution in the Canadas.* Toronto: N C Press, 1974.

Morris, Richard B. *Encyclopedia of American History.* New York: Harper & Brothers, 1953.

Nelson, S. B. *Nelson's Biographical Dictionary and Historical Reference Book of Erie County, Pennsylvania, 1896.* Erie, PA: S. B. Nelson, 1896.

Prothero, Frank and Nancy. *Tales of the North Shore.* Nan-Sea Publications, 1987.

Ratigan, William. *Great Lakes Shipwrecks & Survivals.* New York: Galahad Books, 1960.

Read, Daphne. *The Great War and Canadian Society, An Oral History.* Toronto: New Hogtown Press, 1978.

Senior, Heweward. *The Last Invasion of Canada.* Toronto: Dundurn Press. 1991.

Shipley, Robert, and Fred Addis. *Wrecks and Disasters.* St. Catharines, Ontario: Vanwell, 1992.

Sobol, Ken and Julie Macfie. *Looking for Lake Erie.* Toronto: Viking, Toronto, 1995.

Stone, Dave. *Long Point: Last Port of Call.* Erin, Ontario: Boston Mills Press, 1988.

The Canadian Encyclopedia. Hurtig Publishers, Ltd., 1986.

Thompson, Harold W. *Body, Boots, & Britches.* New York: Dover Publications, 1939.

Tiessen, Ronald. A Bicycle Guide to Pelee Island. Pelee Island Heritage Centre, 1992.

Waldman, Carl. *Atlas of the North American Indian.* New York/Oxford: Facts on File, 1985.

"War on the Great Lakes." *Northwest Ohio Quarterly* 60, no. 4 (1988).

Williamson, Ronald F., and Robert I. MacDonald. *Legacy of Stone.* Toronto: Eastendbooks, 1998.

WPA Writers' Program. *The Michigan Guide.* New York: Oxford University Press, 1941.

WPA Writers' Program. *The Ohio Guide.* New York: Oxford University Press, 1940.

SOURCE NOTES

Introduction:

The John Maynard reference is from The Mariposa Bank Mystery in *Sunshine Sketches of a Little Town* by Stephen Leacock (Toronto: McClelland & Stewart, 1912).

All Anna Jameson quotes from *Winter Studies and Summer Rambles in Canada,* numerous reprint editions.

For more on the ancient Mississippi trading network, see *Native Americans Before 1492,* Lynda Norene Shaffer (Armonk, N.Y.: M.E. Sharpe, 1992).

For research on early Great Lakes water levels, conducted by a University of Colorado team led by Troy Holcombe, see article by Martin Mittelstaedt, The Globe and Mail, May 19, 1999.

Catfish Creek dig reference is from Ontario Archaelogy 63, 1997, by Robert Pihl and Stephen Cox Thomas.

1,000-year-old skeleton reference from Ontario Archaelogy, 57, 1994, "The Shaman of Long Point," by William A. Fox and J. Eldon Molto.

Long Point Burial Goods, Ontario Archaelogy 29, 1978, "The Bruce Boyd Site," by Michael W. Spence, Ronald F. Williamson, and John, H. Dawkins.

Chapter 2:

Land grant figures from *Ohio Lands,* Thomas A. Burke, Ohio Auditor of State, 1993.

"It is a pretty thing . . ." quote from The Pioneer Farmer and Backwoodsman by Edwin C. Guillet (Toronto: Ontario Publishing Co. Ltd., 1963, distributed by University of Toronto Press).

"Fenian Marching Song" from *The Last Invasion of Canada* by Hereward Senior (Toronto: Dundurn Press, 1991).

Chapter 3:

All Jefferson quotes from *Jefferson in His Time*, Dumas Malone, 6 Vol. (Boston: Little, Brown, 1948–81).

DeWitt Clinton quote from *Lake Erie*, by Harlan Hatcher (Bobbs Merrill, 1945).

Eyewitnesss account of the Erie Canal opening quoted in the pamphlet "A History of the City of Tonawanda," by Willard B. Dittmar (Buffalo, 1971) and the Erie County Historical Society.

Lathers letter from Macfie family papers in Dearborn Historical Museum. (John Lathers is Julie Macfie Sobol's great-grandfather)

All Dickens quotes from American Notes, numerous reprint editions.

"Come all ye bold sailors" appears in *The Folk Songs of North America* by Alan Lomax (Garden City, N.Y.: Doubleday & Co. Inc., 1960).

Chapter 4:

UEL land grant figures from Edwin C. Guillet, *The Pioneer Farmer and Backwoodsman* (Toronto: Ontario Publishing Co. Ltd, 1963).

Quote on Port Stanley picnics from interview with Honnie Busch in Cleveland, 2002.

The "Royal Canadians." Given that the Lombardos were Italian immigrants, and as far from royalty as possible, the name always got a good laugh from family and friends. In another of those surprising cross-border coincidences, we discovered, talking to Honnie Busch, that her family and the Lombardos had become friendly after both had moved to Cleveland.

"Soldiers of Canada" by Mrs. Verne Whitman is from the authors' collection of early sheet music.

Port Colborne smuggling statistics from a display at the Port Colborne Historical and Marine Museum.

Chapter 5:

George Washington quote is from *Pioneer Farmer and Backwoodsman*.

Quotation in caption, "They said, is this Canada," is from *Sketches in the History of the Underground Railroad*, published by E. M. Pettit.

Song, "I Am on My Way to Canada," appeared in The Traveler Magazine, 1837, and has been credited to George Clark.

Chapter 7:

Song, "We Leaves Detroit Behind Us," from *Great Lakes Shipwrecks and Survivals* by William Ratigan (Grand Rapids, MI: William B. Eerdmans Publishing, 1977)

Perry and Harrison quotes from an article in Northwest Ohio Quarterly 60, no. 4.

Quote from Johnny Green from *Erie Wrecks East*, Georgann and Michael Wachter, Corporate Impact, Avon Lake, Ohio, 2000.

Chapter 8:

Quote about rope boys from an interview with Douglas Flood, 2001.

The Benny Goodman pictures were snapped by Reg Saville, saxophonist with the Thomas band.

City of Detroit III statistics are from a copy of the contractor's specifications Book, found at the Great Lakes Historical Society, Vermilion, Ohio.

Seeandbee specifications also from Great Lakes Historical Society.

Chapter 9:

Fish recipe appears in *Legacy of Stone* by Ronald Williamson and Robert MacDonald.

The Jack Miner letter is cited in *In Search of a Heart* by Henrietta O'Neill (Leamington, Ontario: Friends of Point Pelee Press, 1999).

INDEX

CONTENTS

Knitting Needles and Other Tools

Knitting needles are made of aluminum, plastic, bamboo, or wood and come in a range of sizes and styles.

The diameter of the needle determines the size of the stitch. Sizes are stated in metric measurements as well as a U.S. numbering system, as given in the chart at right. In general, smaller needles are used for knitting finer yarns, larger needles for heavier yarns.

There are also different types of needles. Straight needles come in different lengths and have a stop on one end to keep stitches from sliding off. This style is used for knitting back and forth in rows, as for a scarf or pieces of a sweater. Double-pointed needles are short with points on both ends, useful for knitting in the round on projects like socks and mittens. Circular needles are two needle points connected by a flexible cable. The points come in the usual range of needle sizes, and they also come in various cable lengths; the longer the cable, the more stitches it will hold. Besides knitting in the round, as for a one-piece sweater, circular needles are also useful for knitting in rows on large projects like blankets.

Other useful items include stitch markers, stitch counters, stitch holders, and yarn bobbins for color work.

KNITTING NEEDLE SIZES

Metric Size	U.S. Size
2.25 mm	1
2.75 mm	2
3.25 mm	3
3.5 mm	4
3.75 mm	5
4 mm	6
4.5 mm	7
5 mm	8
5.5 mm	9
6 mm	10
6.5 mm	10½
8 mm	11
9 mm	13
10 mm	15
12.75 mm	17
15 mm	19
19 mm	35
25 mm	50

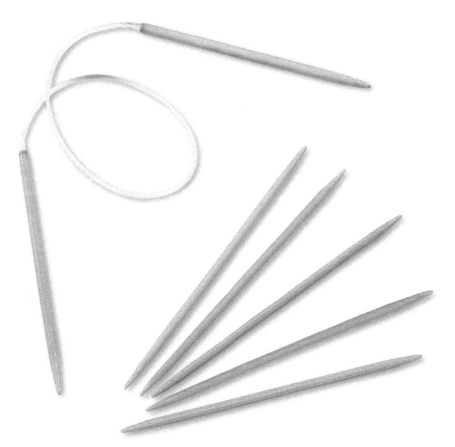

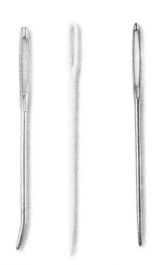

Small sharp scissors for cutting yarn and a flexible tape measure are essential for knitting. For finishing your projects, you will need a yarn or tapestry needle with a blunt end for weaving in yarn ends and hand-sewing seams.

Knitting Instructions

Knitting instructions are written in a shortened form, using standard abbreviations. This greatly reduces the space and overwhelming confusion that would result if the instructions were written out completely, word for word. Sometimes, stitch charts with symbols are included to help you understand the pattern. This happens especially when you are knitting something with cables (page 171) or intarsia (page 221).

Reading Written Instructions

Knitting patterns are often groups of stitches that are repeated a certain number of times in a row or round. Rather than repeat the instructions for the stitch group over and over, the group is enclosed between parentheses or brackets immediately followed by the number of times to work the stitches.

For example: (k2tog, sl 1, k1, psso) 3 times or [k2tog, sl 1, k1, psso] 3 times.

This is a much shorter way to say "knit 2 together, slip 1, knit 1, pass slipped stitch over; knit 2 together, slip 1, knit 1, pass slipped stitch over; knit 2 together, slip 1, knit 1, pass slipped stitch over."

Another way to indicate repeated stitch patterns is with asterisks. This same instruction could be written: * k2tog, sl 1, k1, psso, repeat from * two times more.

Parentheses are also used to clarify or reinforce information. They may be used at the end of a row to tell you how many total stitches you should have in that row, such as (25 sts). Sometimes this information is set off with an em dash at the row end—25 sts. Parentheses are also used to tell you which side of the work you should be on: (WS) or (RS). For multi-size patterns, parentheses enclose the variations you must apply to the different sizes. For example, a pattern may include directions for size 2 (4, 6, 8). Throughout the instructions, wherever you must choose for the correct size, the choices will be written like this: K34 (36, 38, 40).

Abbreviations

Here is the list of standard abbreviations used for knitting. Until you can readily identify them, keep the list handy whenever you knit.

beg . . . . begin

bet . . . . between

BO . . . . bind off

CC . . . . contrasting color

cm . . . . centimeter

cn . . . . cable needle

CO . . . . cast on

Col. . . . . color

cont . . . . continue

dec . . . . decrease

dpn . . . . double-pointed needle(s)

g . . . . grams

inc . . . . increase

k . . . . knit

k1f&b . . . . . . knit into front and back loop of same stitch

k2tog . . . . . knit two stitches together

kwise . . . . . . knitwise

m(s) . . . . markers(s)

MC . . . . main color

rem . . . . remaining or remain

rep . . . . repeat

mm . . . . millimeters

M1 . . . . make one stitch (increase)

oz . . . . ounce

p . . . . purl

p1f&b . . . . . . purl into front and back loop of same stitch

p2tog . . . . . purl two stitches together

patt . . . . pattern

pm . . . . place marker

psso . . . . pass slipped stitch over

pwise . . . . . . purlwise

rep . . . . repeat

rev St st. . . . . reverse stockinette stitch

rib . . . . ribbing

rnd(s) . . . . . . rounds

RS . . . . right side

sk . . . . skip

skp . . . . slip 1, knit 1, pass slipped stitch over (decrease)

sl . . . . slip

sl1k . . . . slip one knitwise

sl1p . . . . slip one purlwise

sl st . . . . slip stitch

sm . . . . slip marker

ssk . . . . slip 1, slip 1, knit these 2 stitches together (decrease)

st(s) . . . . stitch(es)

St st . . . . stockinette stitch

tbl . . . . through back loop

tog . . . . together

WS . . . . wrong side

wyb . . . . with yarn in back

wyf. . . . . with yarn in front

yb . . . . yarn back

yf . . . . yarn forward

yo . . . . yarn over needle

* . . . . repeat from *

[ ] . . . . repeat instructions in brackets as directed

( ) . . . . repeat instructions in parentheses as directed

( ) . . . . number of stitches that should be on the needle or across a row

Techniques

These are the basic techniques for knitting. If you are a beginning knitter, use these pages to help you learn to knit and improve your skills. If you are an occasional knitter, refer to this section to refresh your memory about the different stitches and stitch combinations used for shaping your knitting. Even experienced knitters will return to this section for clarification on stitch directions from time to time.

Casting On Stitches

Every knitting project begins by putting a foundation row of stitches on your needle; this is called casting on. There are several different ways to cast on stitches. The standard method—the one used if your pattern doesn't specify another method—is called long-tail cast-on.

Long-Tail Cast-On

Make a slipknot on the needle and hold the needle in your right hand. Put the thumb and index finger of your left hand between the tail and working yarn, the tail around your thumb and the working yarn around your index finger. Use the other fingers of your left hand to hold both strands snugly against your left palm **(1)**. Insert the needle upward through the loop on your thumb **(2)**. Pivot the needle to the right and go over and under the yarn on your index finger, picking up a loop **(3)**. Pull the loop back down through the thumb loop **(4)**. Let your thumb drop out of the loop and immediately wrap the tail yarn back around your thumb. Spread your fingers to snug up the new stitch on the needle **(5)**. Repeat the steps for each stitch.

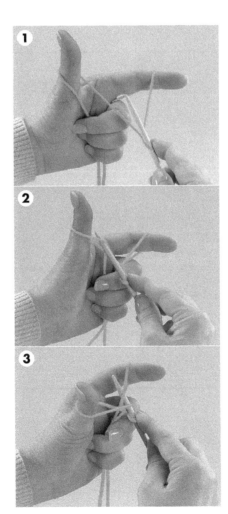

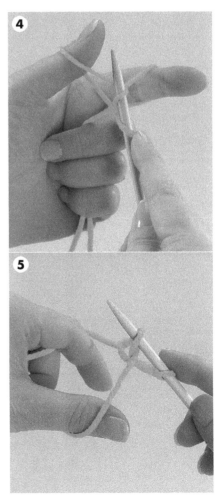

Cable Cast-On

Other cast-on methods are used in specific situations. The cable cast-on is useful if you need to add stitches to your knitting after you've already worked several rows or rounds.

Insert the right needle into the space between the last two stitches on your left needle. Wrap the yarn around your needle (1) and pull a loop through (2). Put this loop back on your left needle. You've just cast on one stitch. Continue in this manner, adding as many stitches as the pattern calls for (3).

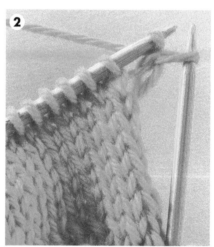

Knit Cast-On

Notice that the knit cast-on is very similar to the cable cast-on. The difference lies in where you insert your needle. This method creates a tight, inelastic edge. Create a slipknot, and place it on your needle to create your first loop. Insert your needle into the loop knitwise. Wrap your yarn around your needle (1) and pull a loop through. Place this loop on your left needle (2). You have just cast-on one stitch. Continue in this manner until you have cast-on the required number of stitches (3).

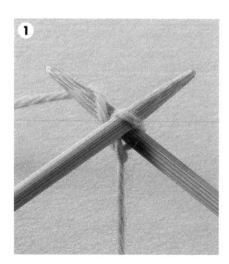

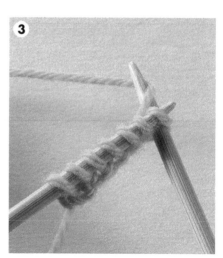

Elastic Cast-On

This method is similar to the long-tail cast-on, but with an extra twist that makes the cast-on row more elastic. Use this method when the cast-on edge needs to stretch, such as for socks, mittens, and hats. Allow extra length (about 30% more) for the yarn tail when casting on with this method.

Make a slipknot on the needle and hold the needle in your right hand. Put the thumb and index finger of your left hand between the tail and working yarn, the tail around your thumb and the working yarn around your index finger. Use the other fingers of your left hand to hold both strands snugly against your left palm **(1)**. Wrap the needle from the front under both strands of the tail yarn **(2)**, insert the tip over the back strand and into the loop between the strands **(3)**. With the back strand still on the needle, bring the needle tip toward you under and over the front strand **(4)**. Catch the working yarn, wrapping it counter-clockwise around the needle **(5)**, bring the needle tip forward and manueuver it back through the thumb loop. Drop the loop from your thumb. Catch the tail yarn with your thumb again, forming a new loop as you snug up the new stitch on the needle **(6)**. Repeat the steps to add stitches **(7)**. Notice the extra bead of yarn under each stitch.

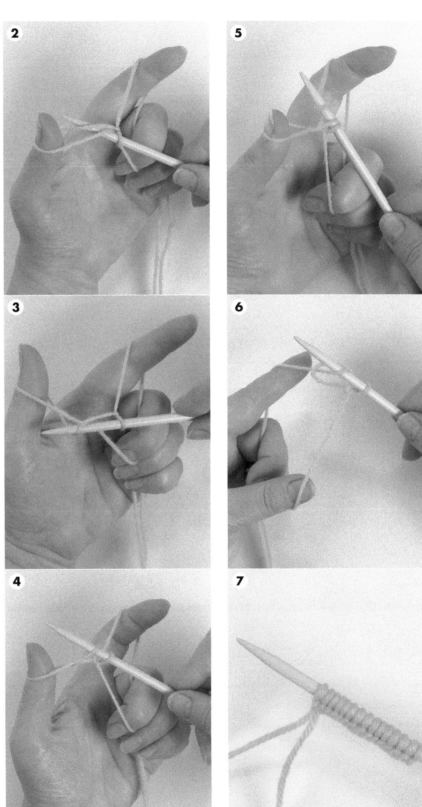

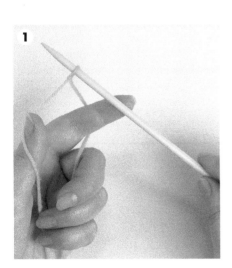

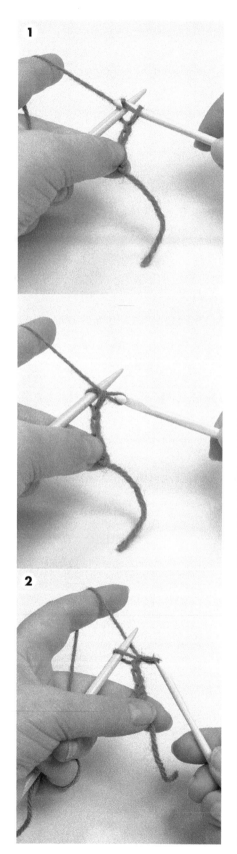

Provisional Cast-On

A provisional cast-on is a way of casting on stitches so that the cast on row can later be removed, leaving a row of "live" stitches that can be placed on a needle and knitted in the opposite direction. There are many uses for this cast-on and many patterns call for it. There are also several ways to achieve a provisional cast-on. My favorite is to use a crochet hook to put the stitches on the needle. It is quite easy to do, and easy to remove the provisional yarn when done.

With a contrasting yarn, make a slip knot, then chain 2 or 3 stitches with crochet hook. Hold a knitting needle in your left hand over the working yarn that is coming from the crochet hook in your right hand. Take the hook over the needle, wrap the yarn over the hook, and pull it through the loop on the hook, making a chain (**1**). Reposition the working yarn under the needle (**2**), and make another stitch over the needle. Continue until you have made the required number of stitches. Chain two or three stitches with just the crochet hook, cut the yarn, and pull the end through (**3**). Make a knot in the beginning tail, so that you know to pull the end without the knot when it comes time to unravel the provisional cast on. Drop the contrast yarn and, starting with the first row, knit the stitches with your project yarn. When you are ready to knit from the cast-on edge, release the stitches of the contrast yarn and pick up the live stitches with your knitting needle (**4**).

Knitting and Purling

Knit the Standard Way

To knit the standard way, (abbreviated k) insert your right needle through the last loop on your left needle from left to right, wrap the yarn around your right needle counter-clockwise **(1)**, and pull a loop through, simultaneously dropping the stitch off of your left needle **(2)**.

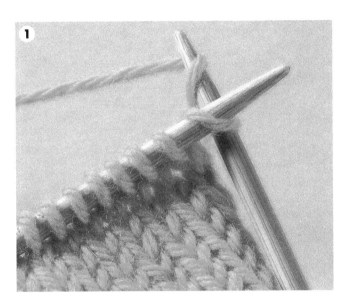

Knit Through Back Loop

To knit through the back loop (ktbl) insert your right needle through the last loop on your left needle from right to left **(3)**. The resulting stitch looks like a knit stitch but is tight and twisted **(4)**.

Purl the Standard Way

Bring your yarn to the front of the work, insert your needle right-to-left through the last loop on your left needle, wrap the yarn around the needle counter-clockwise **(1)**, and pull a loop through onto your right needle while dropping the old loop off your left needle **(2)**.

Purl Through Back Loop

To create a stitch that is twisted from the purl side, purl the stitch through the back loop (abbreviated ptbl). Insert your needle left-to-right through the last loop of your left needle **(3)** and continue to make a purl stitch in the same way **(4)**.

Sl1 purlwise

Sl1 knitwise

Slipping Stitches

To slip a stitch, move your stitch from the left needle to right needle without doing anything to it. When you slip a stitch by inserting your right needle right-to-left into the other stitch (the same way you would if you were going to purl that stitch), you are slipping a stitch purlwise (sl 1 pwise). If you slip a stitch by inserting your needle through it from left-to-right (the way you would if you were going to knit that stitch), you are slipping the stitch knitwise (sl 1 kwise).

Binding Off

Finishing the last row or round of a knitted project so that it will not ravel is called binding off. In the conventional method of binding off, usually done from the right side, you knit the first two stitches, then, using your left needle, lift the second stitch on the right needle up and over the stitch that you've just knit. One stitch is bound off. Repeat this, once stitch at a time until all stitches are bound off. When a pattern just tells you to bind off all stitches, this is the method to use. If the pattern tells you to bind off in pattern, you knit or purl each stitch following the stitch pattern that has been established before binding it off.

Purl Two Together Bind-Off

You can also bind off from the wrong side, or purl side of stockinette stitching. For this common method of binding-off, purl two stitches together **(1)**, transfer this stitch back to your left needle **(2)**, and purl two stitches again **(3)**. Repeat this operation until you've bound off the required number of stitches.

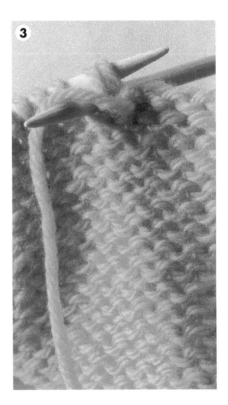

Three-Needle Bind-Off

Three-needle bind-off method finishes two edges and joins them together at once. This is especially useful for shoulder seams of sweaters. Both needles must hold the same number of stitches. A third needle is used to bind them off and together.

Hold the two pieces that you're joining with their right sides facing each other. Then, insert a third needle knitwise through the first stitch on the front needle and through the first stitch on the back needle **(1)**. Wrap the yarn around the tip of your needle, and pull a loop through both stitches as you simultaneously drop the stitches from the front and back needles **(2)**. Repeat these steps to get a second stitch onto your right needle. Once you have two stitches on your right needle, use the tip of the left needle to lift the second stitch on your right needle up and over the first stitch **(3)**, thus binding off one stitch. Continue in this way to the end of the row.

Picot Bind-Off

The picot bind-off creates a decorative edge and can be used on edges that will not be seamed, such as neck or front borders, baby clothes and blankets.

Use the basic knit method, bind off the first 2 stitches, *turn, using knit cast-on method, cast on 3 additional stitches, turn, bind off all but one of the stitches by passing the second over the first till 1 stitch remains on right needle, bind off 2 more stitches, repeat from * till end of row.

Shaping

When you sew, you shape fabric with darts or tucks or simply in the way you cut the garment pieces. There are various ways to shape fabric as you knit: decreasing or increasing the number of stitches on the needle, and adding short rows into the work. Basically, adding another row or round increases the length of a shape. Increasing or decreasing the number of stitches in a row alters the width of the shape. Adding short rows causes portions of the shape to curve forward or backward.

Decreasing

Here are various ways to decrease the number of stitches. Each method has a distinct appearance.

Knit Two Together (k2tog)

Knitting two stitches together has a definite orientation: it is right-leaning. The stitch on the left always leans to the right and sits on top of the stitch on the right. Insert needle knitwise into two stitches together, wrap the yarn around the needle (1), pull the loop through (2).

Slip-Slip-Knit (ssk)

To create a left-leaning decrease that mirrors knitting two stitches together is slip-slip-knit. Slip the two stitches knitwise, one at a time (1), (2), and insert your left needle into them to knit them together. You have decreased one stitch and the right stitch leans on top of the left stitch.

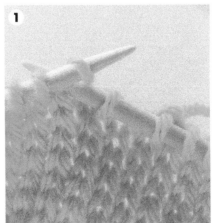

Purl Two Together (p2tog)

To create a right-leaning decrease from the wrong side of the work, purl two stitches together: insert the right needle into two stitches purlwise, wrap yarn around tip of right needle (**1**), and pull a loop through (**2**).

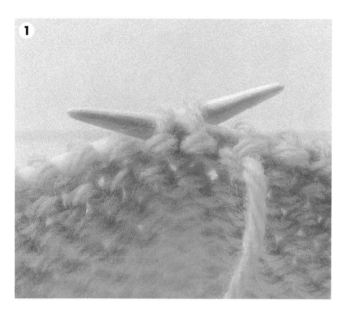

Purl Two Together Through Back Loops (p2tog-tbl)

To create a left-leaning decrease from the wrong side of the work, purl two stitches together through their back loops. Take your right needle, and, turning the work slightly to see the backside, insert it left-to-right through your two stitches. Then, wrap your yarn around the tip of your right needle (**1**), and, with as few expletives as possible, pull a loop through onto your right needle (**2**).

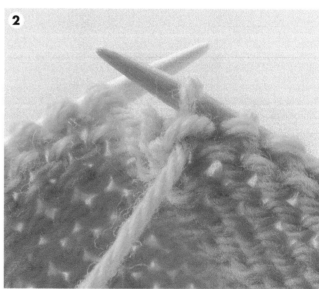

Increasing

Each of these different increase methods looks different, and is suitable for a different situation.

Bar Increase (kfb)

This is one of the simplest increases. Instructions may tell you to knit into front and back loop of same stitch. The new stitch that you create with this method will have a little bar at its base, which will be highly visible. Often, the bar increase is used in situations where the bar blends in with the rest of the stitches (as in garter stitch) or when the bar serves a decorative function to highlight the line at which you are increasing stitches.

Knit a stitch, but don't drop it off your left needle **(1)**. Now, insert your right needle into the back loop of the stitch **(2)**, and knit it again, now allowing the stitch to slide off your left needle **(3)**. Your single stitch will now have become two, with the second stitch branching from a little horizontal bar.

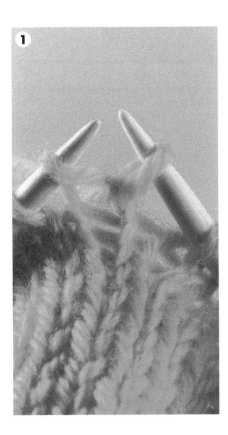  

Make One Increases (M1R and M1L)

Make one increases are nearly invisible. To perform both the right and left versions of the make one increase, you pick up the running yarn between your needles, place it on your left needle, and knit into it. How you place the running yarn on your left needle and how you knit into the resulting loop varies, based on whether you are working the right or the left version of the increase.

Make One Right (M1R)

Unlike decreases, which clearly have a direction in which they slant, increases have a slant that's much more subtle. The right-leaning version of the make-one increase, abbreviated M1R, tends to be the default make-one increase to use. If the instructions simply say M1, use this method. Insert your right needle under the running yarn from front to back **(1)**. Then, transfer the resulting loop onto your left needle **(2)**. Now, knit into this loop in the normal way, thereby adding an extra stitch to your row **(3)**.

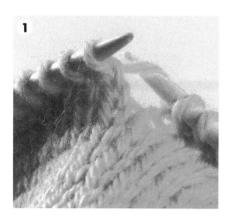
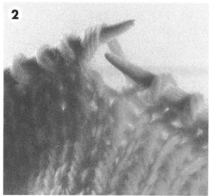
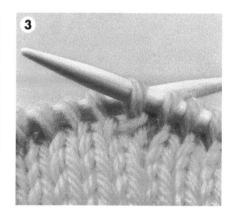

Make One Left (M1L)

To work the left version of the make-one increase, insert your left needle under the running yarn from front to back, transfer the loop to your left needle **(1)**. Now, knit into the back loop of this stitch, once again adding an extra stitch to your row.

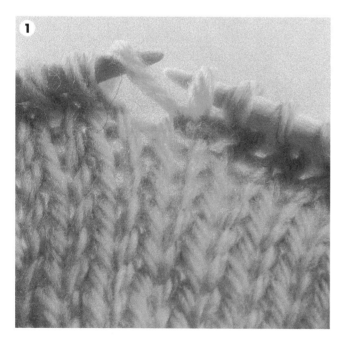

Note the subtle difference in the way these increases slant.

Lifting Up the Loop Increases (krl and kll)

To work loop increases, add an extra stitch by knitting into the head of the stitch in the row below the one you are working.

Right Loop Increase (krl)

To work the right version, use your right needle to lift up the head of the stitch that's directly below the stitch on your left needle **(1)**. Place this loop on your left needle **(2)** and knit into it **(3)**, thereby adding an extra stitch to your row.

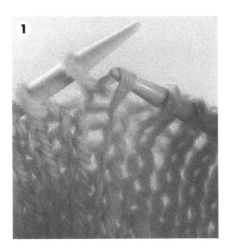 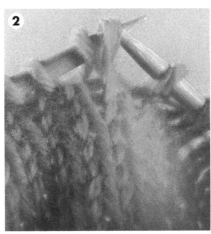 

Left Loop Increase (kll)

To work the left version of the loop increase, use your left needle to lift up the head of the stitch that's two stitches below the stitch on your right needle **(1)**. Keep this loop on your left needle. Then knit into this loop **(2)**, adding an extra stitch to your row.

 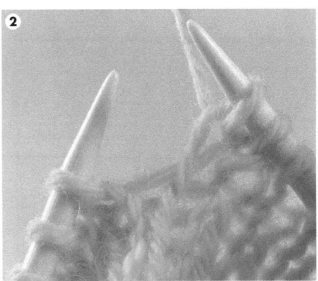

Yarn Over Increase (yo)

The yarn-over increase, used often in knitting lace, creates a hole in the fabric. Bring your yarn forward, wrap it, counterclockwise, around the right needle and return it to the back of the work **(1)**. In the next row, knit or purl this wrap like any other stitch. The yarn over increase leaves a hole **(2)**.

Short Rows

A short row is exactly what it sounds like: a row that you add into your knitting that has fewer stitches than the number of stitches on your needle. Instead of knitting all the stitches on the needle, you knit only some of them, turn your knitting, and purl back to the beginning of your row, thus adding a short row into your knitting.

If you add short rows to one side of your knitting, you are making one selvage of the work longer than the other selvage.

If you add short rows to the center of your knitting, you are making the central length of your work longer than the selvage length. This will result in a central bulge.

Short rows on one side

Short rows in the center

Wrapping and Turning (w&t)

If you worked the short row as described above, you would create a hole at the junction between the short row and the rest of your knitting. To avoid making a hole, perform an operation called wrapping and turning (abbreviated w&t). Instead of knitting your short row and simply turning, knit your short row, wrap your yarn around the following unworked stitch, and only then turn and work back to the beginning of the row. How you wrap and turn depends on whether you are working on the knit side or the purl side of stockinette stitch fabric.

Wrap and Turn from Knit Side

When working a short row on the knit side of the fabric, knit the required number of stitches, bring the yarn forward to the front of your work, slip the next (unworked) stitch from our left needle to our right needle **(1)**, bring the yarn to the back of your work, and slip the unworked stitch back to our left needle **(2)**. Now turn the knitting and purl back to the beginning **(3)**.

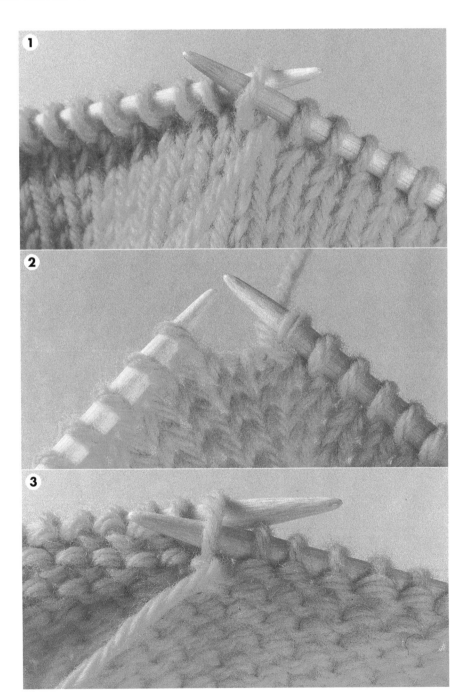

Wrap and Turn from Purl Side

When working a short row on the purl side of the fabric, bring the yarn to the back of the work, slip the next unworked stitch from the left needle to the right needle **(1)**, bring the yarn to the front of the work again, and slip the unworked stitch back to the left needle **(2)**. Then, you're ready to turn and work the next row **(3)**.

Taking Care of Wraps

When you wrap and turn, you are left with some unsightly little bars that highlight where you turned the short row. To make the bar less visible, lift the bar onto the left needle and work it together with the next stitch. Most patterns don't include notes on when you'll be passing these wraps, so you have to watch for them.

Purling Wrap with Stitch

When you pass a wrap on the purl side of the fabric (the wrong side in stockinette stitch), insert your right needle front-to-back under the wrap **(1)** and place it onto your left needle, allowing it to sit on the right of the stitch around which it was wrapped **(2)**. Then, purl the stitch and its wrap together **(3)**. Though this will produce a bulbous yarn loop on the purl side of the fabric, you'll notice that the wrap will disappear from the knit side of the fabric, leaving an even, neat knit stitch **(4)**.

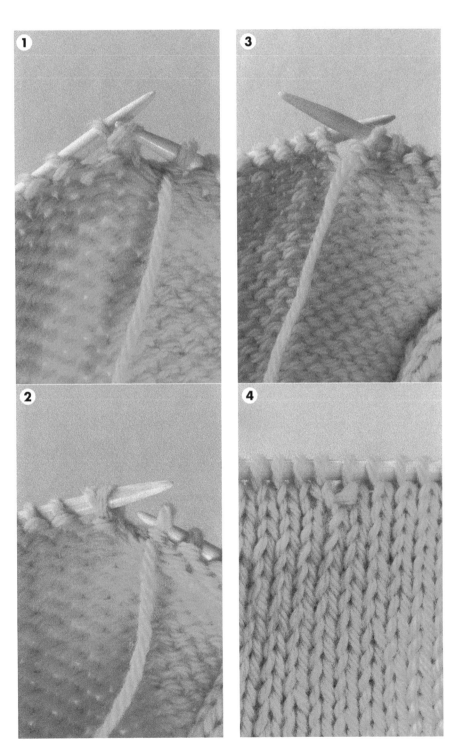

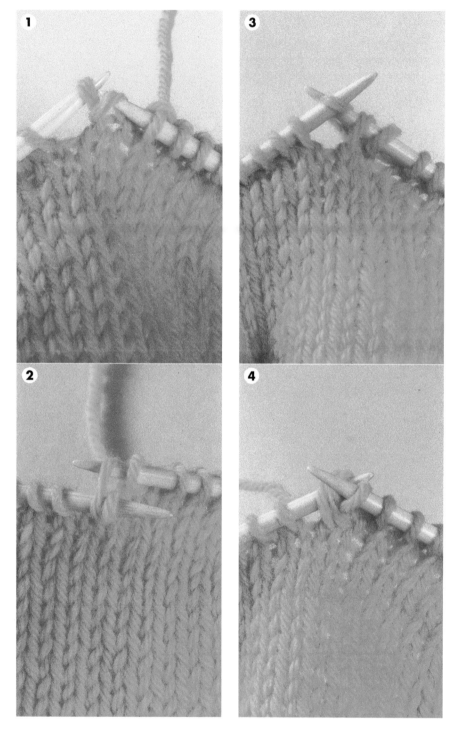

Knitting Wrap with Stitch

When you pass a wrap on the knit side of the fabric, first insert your right needle front-to-back under the wrap **(1)**. Then, lift the wrap onto your left needle, up and over the stitch that it was wrapped around **(2)**. Slip first the stitch and then the wrap knitwise **(3)**, and then knit them together **(4)**. Note that this final step of slipping twice and knitting together is nearly identical to the slip-slip-knit (ssk) decrease.

Knitting in the Round

Sometimes it is necessary to knit in a tubular shape, going around in circles. This can be done in different ways: using one circular needle, using four or five double-pointed needles, or using two circular needles. Which method you use depends on how many stitches there are in the circle. If all the stitches fit comfortable (without stretching) on the cable of a circular needle, you can use one circular needle. Tubes with fewer stitches than will fit on the cable of a circular needle can be knit on double pointed needles, dividing the stitches among three or four needles and knitting them consecutively with another needle. You can also knit in the round with two circular needles, dividing the stitches between them and alternating from one needle to the other.

Using Double-Pointed Needles

To begin knitting a tube on double-pointed needles, cast on the required number of stitches that form the initial circumference of your tube onto a single needle. Then divide these stitches evenly onto three or four double-pointed needles (**1**) and arrange the needles in a circle, being careful not to twist your stitches (**2**). Use an extra needle and the yarn coming from the final stitch that you cast on to begin working the first cast on stitch, the first stitch of your round. A great way to keep your first stitch firmly attached to your final stitch in your circle is to knit the first three stitches of your round with both your working yarn and the long yarn tail from your cast-on stitches (**3**). Knit the rest of the stitches from needle one, using only the working yarn. Use the empty needle to continue knitting the stitches on the next needle in your round. Continue in this manner, and you'll soon have a tube-shaped piece of knitting (**4**).

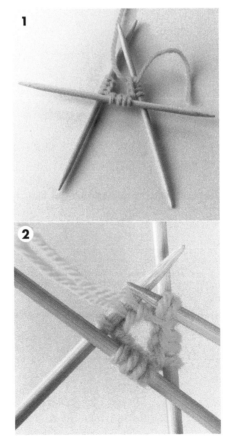

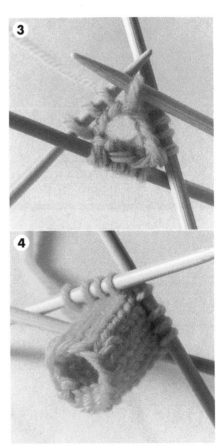

Knitting a Tube with One Circular Needle

Make sure you choose a circular needle with a cable long enough to hold all the stitches. Cast on all the stitches and distribute them along the cable (taking care not to twist your stitches) until the first stitch reaches the opposite point. Hold the tip with the last cast-on stitch in your right hand and the tip with the beginning stitch in your left hand. Use the yarn coming from the final cast-on stitch to begin working the first cast-on stitch, the first stitch of your round. Knit all the stitches in the round, shifting them along the cable as you go. Although the yarn tail indicates where each round begins, you may want to place a stitch marker at the beginning stitch as an extra reminder.

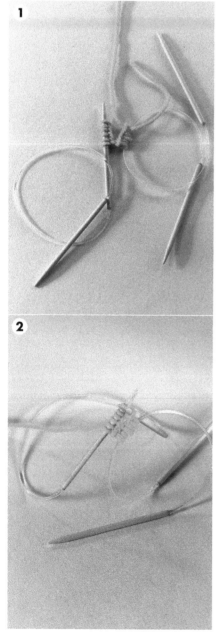

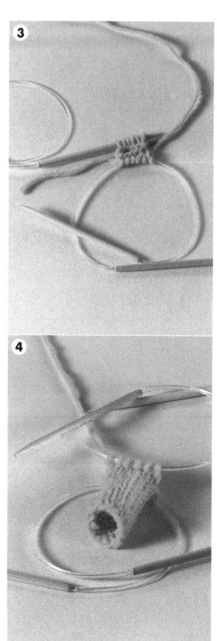

Knitting a Tube on Two Circular Needles

When you knit a tube on two circular needles, you work from only one needle at a time, so you'll always have one working needle and one idle needle. Stitches on the resting circular needle hang loosely on the cable portion of the needle.

To begin, cast on the stitches for the circumference of your tube onto one circular needle. Transfer half the stitches (beginning with the slipknot) onto the second circular needle, and slide these stitches to the opposite tip of that needle (**1**). Slide the stitches on needle one to the center of the needle cable, and drop needle one. Using the free tip of needle two, join the stitches into a round, working the first three stitches of your round with both the working yarn and the yarn tail from the cast-on end held together (**2**). Finish knitting the rest of the stitches on that needle, using only the working yarn. Then slide all the stitches on needle two to the center of the needle cable (**3**). Drop needle two and pick up needle one. Push the stitches from the cable to the tip of the needle. Then, use the opposite end of needle one, knit all the stitches on that needle. Drop needle one and pick up needle two. Continue this process, alternating between needles, until you've finished your tube (**4**).

I-cord

Some tubes can be knit using only two double-point needles. These tubes are known as idiot cord, or merely I-cord. Any tube that has five stitches or less in circumference can be worked as I-cord.

Cast-on or pick up the required number of stitches on a double-pointed needle. Knit the stitches with another double-pointed needle, but don't turn the work. Slide the stitches to the opposite end of the needle **(1)**. Pull the working yarn tight across the back of the stitches **(2)** and knit another row. Repeat this many times, forming a tiny knitted tube **(3)**. To keep the stitches looking uniform, tug on the tube every few rows.

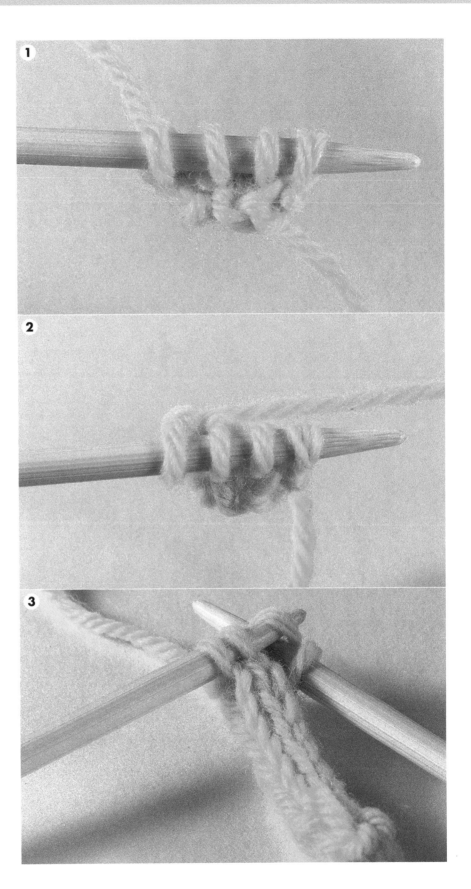

Checking Your Gauge

Gauge refers to the number of stitches and the number of rows in a given width and length of knitted fabric, usually in 4-inch (10 cm) increments. Before knitting a project, check the gauge to ensure your stitching creates the correct denseness of weave.

Every pattern indicates the exact yarn (or weight of yarn) and size needles to use and the finished measurements of the project shown. Yarn labels also list the needle size and recommended gauge for that yarn. It is important to choose yarn in the weight specified for the project to successfully complete the project. The needle size recommended is the size an average knitter would use to get the correct gauge.

Unfortunately, many knitters don't fall in the average range. Some of us knit tighter, others looser. To check your gauge, use the yarn and needle called for in the instructions to cast on the number of stitches indicated by the gauge in the

pattern plus four more stitches. For example, if the gauge is 16 stitches = 4" (10 cm), cast on 20 stitches. Work the pattern stitch, keeping two stitches at each end in knit, until you have an approximate 4" (10 cm) square. Lay the swatch flat and measure your swatch from side to side between the two edge stitches. If the swatch is 4" (10 cm) wide, you are knitting to the correct gauge. If the swatch is smaller than 4" (10 cm), you need to use a larger needle; if it is larger than 4" (10 cm), you need to use a smaller needle. Don't try to change your personal knitting style; just change your needle size and knit another swatch.

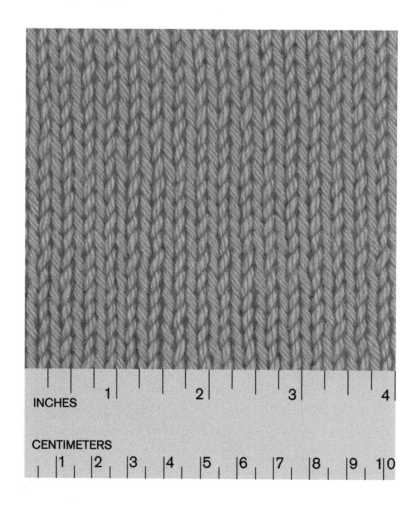

Details and Finishing Techniques

For any project, the quality of the detail work will determine the success of that project. There are various ways to sew seams, pick up stitches, add pockets, or sew in zippers. Here are some techniques for getting the details right every time.

Seaming

Seaming is necessary in nearly any sort of knitting. Different seam methods are used for different circumstances. The following types of seaming are the most common types. For any type of seaming, use a blunt-end yarn or tapestry needle.

Whip Stitch

To whip stitch a seam, hold the pieces with wrong sides facing each other, and push your threaded needle through both pieces. Take the next stitch close to the first one, inserting the needle from the same side as the first stitch. The yarn will wrap over the top of the seam. Repeat to the end of the seam.

Mattress Stitch

Mattress stitch is an invisible seaming stitch, useful for attaching two pieces together by their selvages. Lay the pieces edge-to-edge, right side up. Hook your threaded tapestry needle under the first two running yarns between the selvage and the first column of stitches on one of the pieces. Then, insert your needle under the first two running yarns between the first column of stitches and selvage on the second piece. Zigzag back and forth like this, catching every two rows in turn. Leave the stitches fairly loose. After every few stitches, gently pull the yarn to tighten the seam and bring the edges together.

Fake Grafting

Fake grafting allows you to connect cast-on edges to bound-off edges, cast-on edges to other cast-on edges, and bound-off edges to other bound-off edges. To begin, place the pieces edge-to-edge, right side up. Hook the needle around the first column of stitches in the first piece, then under the first column of stitches in the second piece. Continue in this manner. Note that when you hook the needle under a column of stitches, the column must "point" toward the seam itself. In other words, hook the needle around the base of a knit stitch (bottom of the V) rather than around the top of the knit stitch (the top of the V).

Combination Seaming

Pieces do not always align columns to columns or rows to rows. Often you need to seam two pieces together with rows to columns. Use a combination of mattress stitch and fake grafting to attach the pieces together.

Kitchener Stitch

Kitchener stitch, also known as grafting, is the seaming method of choice when you need to join a row of live stitches to a second row of live stitches. It produces an invisible seam that's virtually undetectable. Cut the working yarn, leaving a tail about 18" (46 cm) long. Leave the stitches on the needles; there should be the same number of stitches on each. Hold the needles side by side in the left hand, with the right side facing up. Slide the stitches toward the needle tips.

The working yarn will be coming from the first stitch on the back needle. To help demonstrate the steps, a contrasting yarn has been used in the photos. Thread the yarn tail on a yarn needle. Draw the yarn through the first stitch on the front needle as if to purl, and leave the stitch on the needle (**1**).

Keeping the yarn under the needles, draw the yarn through the first stitch on the back needle as if to knit, and leave the stitch on the needle (**2**).

* Draw the yarn through the first stitch on the front needle as if to knit, and slip the stitch off the needle (**3**). Draw the yarn through the next stitch on the front needle as if to purl, and leave the stitch on the needle.

Draw the yarn through the first stitch on the back needle as if to purl, and slip the stitch off the needle (**4**). Draw the yarn through the next stitch on the back needle as if to knit, and leave the stitch on the needle.

Repeat from * until all but the last two stitches have been worked off the needles. Insert the tapestry needle knitwise into the stitch on the front needle, and purlwise into the stitch on the back needle, slipping both stitches off their respective needles. Stretch out your seam or use the tip of a needle to adjust stitches a bit to even out the tension in the yarn (**5**).

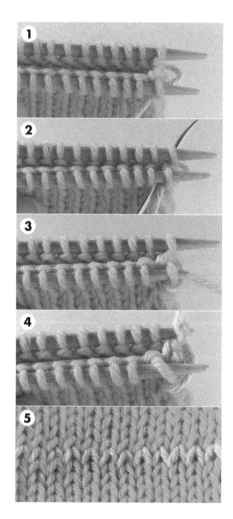

Picking Up Stitches

Picking up stitches from one edge to begin knitting in a new direction is a common technique used in many types of knitting. When knitting a sweater, for example, you might pick up stitches from the neck opening to add a neck band or collar.

To do this, slip your right needle into an available hole along the indicated edge, wrap your yarn around your needle (**1**), and pull a loop through onto your right needle (**2**). Now you've picked up one stitch. Continue in this manner across the edge (or middle) of your work until you've picked up the required number of stitches.

The way you pick up stitches also varies slightly depending on where you are picking up your stitches: from a cast-on or bound-off edge, from a selvage, or from the middle of your fabric.

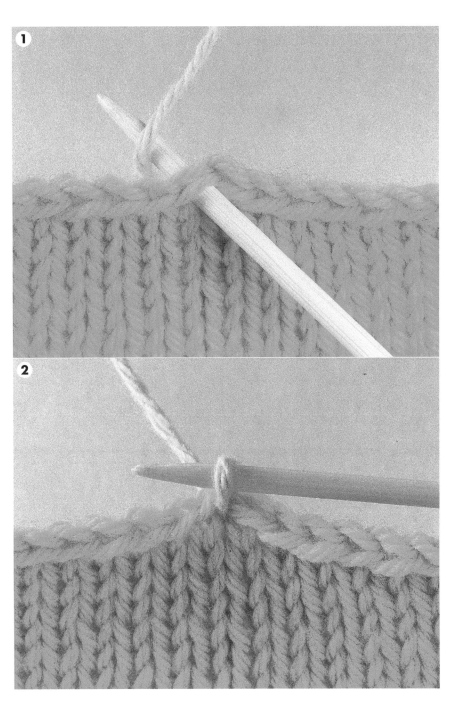

Picking Up Stitches
from a Cast-On Edge

To pick up stitches from a cast-on edge, pick up one stitch per column of stitches. There are two ways to pick up stitches from a cast-on edge. You can pick up stitches invisibly from a cast-on edge by poking your needle between each column directly underneath the yarn strands of the cast-on edge itself **(1)**.

You can also pick up stitches by poking your needle through the loops that are on the other side of the straight edge. This will create a neat line demarcating the edge itself, and is often useful for decorative purposes, where creating a clear line at the edge where you are picking up stitches is an important design element **(2)**.

Picking Up Stitches from a Bound-Off Edge

Picking up stitches from a bound-off edge is almost identical to picking them up from a cast-on edge. Pick up one stitch for every column of stitches on your edge. Pick up stitches invisibly from your edge, or pick them up in such a way that you create a clear demarcating line where you've picked up stitches.

Picking Up Stitches from a Selvage

When knitting in stockinette, the stitches are wider than they are tall. So, picking up stitches along a selvage requires that you pick up approximately three stitches for every four rows along the edge. How to pick up stitches from your selvage varies, depending on what type of selvage you have. Selvages are either a loose chain selvage **(1)**, created by slipping the first stitch of every row, or a tight garter selvage **(2)**, created by knitting or purling the first stitch of every row. The chain selvage is a nice edge for scarves and shawls.

Chain selvage

Garter selvage

When you're picking up stitches along a chain selvage, you will have two rows of stitches per link in your chain. Pick up your stitches as follows: pick up one stitch in-between chains, one stitch at the chain, and another stitch in-between chains. Then, skip the next chain and begin again. Notice the groups of three. With this method, the picked-up stitches will be tightly attached to your selvage.

Picking up stitches along a chain selvage

In a garter selvage, you have one knot per two rows of knitting. To maintain the three-to-four ratio, pick up one stitch between knots, one stitch at a knot, another stitch between knots, and then skip the next knot. The spaces between the knots, as well as the knots themselves, are pretty tight, so as long as you pick up three stitches per four rows of knitting, the junction between your selvage and your new stitches should be relatively hole-free.

Picking up stitches along a garter selvage

CPSIA information can be obtained
at www.ICGtesting.com
Printed in the USA
LVHW071143160721
692796LV00002B/10